THE NORTON SERIES ON
SOCIAL EMOTIONAL LEARNING SOLUTIONS
PATRICIA A. JENNINGS, SERIES EDITOR

*Mindfulness in the Secondary Classroom: A Guide for
Teaching Adolescents*
Patricia C. Broderick

*SEL Every Day: Integrating Social and Emotional Learning
with Instruction in Secondary Classrooms*
Meena Srinivasan

*Assessing Students' Social and Emotional Learning:
A Guide to Meaningful Measurement*
Clark McKown

*Mindfulness in the PreK–5 Classroom:
Helping Students Stress Less and Learn More*
Patricia A. Jennings

*Preventing Bullying in Schools:
A Social and Emotional Learning Approach to Early Intervention*
Catherine P. Bradshaw and Tracy Evian Waasdorp

NORTON BOOKS IN EDUCATION

Advance Praise

"Every educator should read this wonderful, groundbreaking book for practical, research-based guidance to promote the social, emotional, and academic learning of all students. It provides clear, compelling descriptions of beneficial strategies to help teachers (a) create a positive, caring culture that brings out the best in students, (b) teach social and emotional skills with intention, and (c) offer opportunities that motivate students to apply their social and emotional skills to enhance their academic work."

—**Roger P. Weissberg, Ph.D.,** Chief Knowledge Officer and Board Vice Chair, Collaborative for Academic, Social, and Emotional Learning

"Grounded in current and solid research, this book is nonetheless wholly readable, completely practical, and superbly organized. Its conversational tone makes reading *SEL From the Start* feel like a conversation with a trusted colleague. It is not only a trustworthy guide for integrating SEL into primary and elementary classrooms but is also a rich 'course' for teachers for understanding the what, why, and how of social-emotional learning."

—**Carol Ann Tomlinson, Ed.D.,** author of *How to Differentiate Instruction in Academically Diverse Classrooms (3rd Ed.)*

"Too often, social-emotional learning is viewed as something separate from academics. (SEL skills are even sometimes mislabeled as "non-academic.") Or SEL is something done *to* children—systems involving sticker charts come to mind. In *SEL From the Start*, Sara Rimm-Kaufman provides practical guidance for teaching SEL as a part of everyday schoolwork. Grounded in research and real classrooms, this book is a supportive guide for educators as they teach these critical skills to students."

—**Mike Anderson,** education consultant and author of *What We Say and How We Say It Matter*

"With its foundational declaration that SEL is not only what you teach, but how you teach, *SEL From the Start* is a practical, straightforward guide for educators to use in their classrooms. A must-read for any educator serious about supporting the whole child, Rimm-Kaufman reminds us that when learning environments are constructed to teach these skills as mutually reinforcing and central to learning, children are far better equipped to engage learning."

—**Jacqueline Jodl,** Associate Professor, University of Virginia, School of Education and Human Development

SEL From the Start

SEL From the Start

Building Skills in K–5

SARA E. RIMM-KAUFMAN

W. W. NORTON & COMPANY
Independent Publishers Since 1923

The research reported here was supported by the Institute of Education Sciences, U.S. Department of Education, through Grant R305A150272 to the University of Virginia. The opinions expressed are those of the authors and do not represent views of the institute or the U.S. Department of Education.

For information about special discounts for bulk purchases, please contact W. W. Norton Special Sales at specialsales@wwnorton.com or 800-233-4830

Manufacturing by Versa Press
Book design by Molly Heron
Production manager: Katelyn MacKenzie

Library of Congress Cataloging-in-Publication Data

Names: Rimm-Kaufman, Sara, author.
Title: SEL from the start : building skills in K-5 / Sara E. Rimm-Kaufman.
Description: First edition. | New York : W. W. Norton & Company, [2021] |
Series: Norton books in education | Includes bibliographical references and index.
Identifiers: LCCN 2020013212 | ISBN 9780393714609 (paperback) |
ISBN 9780393714616 (epub)
Subjects: LCSH: Affective education. | Education, Elementary. |
Social learning. | Emotional intelligence.
Classification: LCC LB1072 .R55 2021 | DDC 370.15/3—dc23
LC record available at https://lccn.loc.gov/2020013212

W. W. Norton & Company, Inc., 500 Fifth Avenue, New York, N.Y. 10110
www.wwnorton.com

W. W. Norton & Company Ltd., 15 Carlisle Street, London W1D 3BS

1 2 3 4 5 6 7 8 9 0

To my children's teachers

Contents

Acknowledgments xiii

Introduction xvii

1 Develop Classroom Norms 1

2 Teach Active Listening 21

3 Respectful Communication 34

4 Respecting Multiple Perspectives 51

5 Managing Frustration and Anger 74

6   Giving and Receiving Feedback 91

7   Persevering 110

8   Resolving Conflict 127

Conclusion: SEL for the Future 149
References 159
Children's Literature Cited in the Text 165
Index 167

Acknowledgments

As a professor of education for 20 years, I have often asked myself: What if I take my accumulated knowledge and my team's best work and create an SEL book for teachers? I wrote this book as a response to that persistent question. My hope was that it would be easy and fun to read. I pictured teachers scanning the pages as they hovered over a washing machine waiting for the spin cycle to finish.

I began this work in 2014 with Eileen Merritt, assistant professor at the Mary Lou Fulton Teachers College at Arizona State University, and Tracy Harkins, founder of Harkins Consulting, LLC, and codeveloper of KIDS as Planners, an approach to service-learning. Together, we set out to create a service-learning approach that integrated Next Generation Science Standards, high quality service-learning, and instruction in social and emotional skills. We received an Innovation and Development grant from the Institute of Education Sciences with which we launched Connect Science (see https://www.connectscience.org for more information and to join us for an upcoming institute).

This book is based on the lessons on social and emotional learning (SEL) that we created for Connect Science. Our goal with this book was to bring these ideas to the broadest audience possible so that teachers could improve their SEL practices and use these ideas to launch their new school year. At the end of the grant, each of us chose specific aspects of the project to advance. One of my roles has been to prepare this book, and I have fully appreciated the opportunity to revisit SEL lessons and ready them for a new audience.

The ideas in this book emanated from an amazing team of people. Tracy Harkins and Eileen Merritt generated content drawing from their extensive teaching experience, work with teachers, and deep knowledge. Many of the ideas for these lessons were created and developed by Kristen Jones, Mary Beth Anderson, and Ashley Hunt and honed by elementary teachers as well as master's and doctoral students. Mike Anderson, author of *The Well-Balanced Teacher* (2012), led the lesson on classroom norms. Joyce Tugel introduced exciting ideas and helped us see how teachers could use SEL to improve academic instruction. Many people worked long hours to develop and test ideas with teachers including Rebecca McGregor, Candace Lapan, Nicole Bowers, and Julie Thomas. We have been fortunate to have a group of talented master's and undergraduate students including Mary Anna Adams, Beth Armitage, Noah Green, Julia Hahn, Tiffany Hwang, Crystal Keefe, Claire Kirchoff, Anna McAloon, Katie Miller, and Emily Vislosky. A special thank you to Frances Coolman, Robin Fox, and Mollie Lubetkin for their advance read of this book. Thanks to Krystal Thomas for her reflections, as well. I appreciate the encouragement from Patricia Jennings at the University of Virginia to write this book and the careful work of Carol Collins at W. W. Norton to bring this effort to fruition. Thank you to Mariah Eppes and Jamie Vincent for their attentive editing work.

Between 2015 and 2020, we received feedback on these ideas and lessons from over 100 elementary school teachers. These teachers have been crucial in the development and improvement of this work. Teachers have demanding, time-consuming jobs, yet they managed to provide us the kind of feedback we needed to prepare this book. I am grateful to those teachers for their insights and to their administrators for inviting us into their schools. I also appreciate the students and their families for being a part of this work.

Above all, my family motivates me to share my best work with teachers working with children. I am particularly grateful to Sam, Davida, Alan, and Larry. My siblings, nieces, nephews, and kids have all benefited enormously from their many gifted and devoted teachers. My parents, who often say they have lived the American Dream, remember the great teachers that they had 70-plus years ago. My goal with this book is to boost your ability to create a cheery, functioning classroom where students are prepared to work together, talk respectfully to one another, and persevere at challenging academic work. I wish you a productive school year. May your students learn and practice the skills they will need now and in the future.

Introduction

In Ms. Jackson's fourth grade science class, students were learning about energy systems, building circuits, and discussing energy-related problems related to renewable and nonrenewable resources. After some deep conversations about the trade-offs of using different sources of energy, the class discovered a problem that they wanted to solve. The plastic water bottles that they brought from home, used, and then threw away were made from petroleum that was formed hundreds of millions of years ago. They realized if they kept using up nonrenewable resources like petroleum, there would not be enough to use in the future.

The class launched into action to share their new knowledge with their school community. Small groups worked together on different aspects of the project. One group made "Did you know?" posters to hang in the cafeteria to teach students about petroleum and plastic. Another group wrote a short announcement about the project to be included in the morning announcements. Yet another prepared a pledge for students to sign if they would commit to using reusable water bottles. More than 300 students signed the pledge. (Apparently, some kindergarteners and first graders signed more than once. The fourth graders had to do some heady calculations to figure out the actual number of signees.) All of the students in the classroom switched to reusable water bottles, held each other accountable, and bubbled with excitement about their progress and impact.

This anecdote comes from a classroom where students are working together to apply what they learn in science class to a real-world problem in their community. The students are mostly from families with limited financial resources, and many are receiving special education services. This teacher—a cheery, energetic, African American mother of four—began her school year focused on boosting students' social skills. Through a series of lessons in the first few months of school, she created norms and a caring classroom culture. She supported students' ability to listen and speak respectfully to one another, manage strong feelings of frustration, give and receive feedback, and much more. She showed her students that she valued them, and she talked openly about the importance of high-quality relationships, working as a community, and developing the social skills needed to do their best work together. The "empty" minutes in her classroom—transition time at the start of the day, time waiting in line—were far from empty. She infused those moments with conversation about academic ideas, reflection on social experiences, and comments that helped students get excited and curious about learning. Despite knowing that her students could become loud and chaotic, she was comfortable having a productive classroom where things did not always go perfectly but where students learned and practiced the skills they would need to contribute to a better world. This fourth grade teacher taught social and emotional learning (SEL) from the start.

My goal with this book is to help you start your school year well, by laying a solid foundation for building students' social and emotional skills. For the past five years, I have worked with educational content developers and science and service-learning education experts on a project called Connect Science. One part of that work focused on supporting teachers to develop their students' social and emotional skills. The hundred or so teachers we worked with loved this work. We heard repeatedly, "I want to use these ideas to start my year," and "This is the exact content that I need for my classroom right in the beginning of the year," and "In the first few weeks, I like to teach students social skills that they will use all year long—this gives me a perfect road map." I prepared this book in response to those elementary school teachers who craved a better way to start their year.

I fully acknowledge the incredible pressures you experience as a teacher. Classroom management issues and student behavior problems are a constant drain on teachers' energy. Many teachers feel exhausted. New standards and curricula take time to learn and create additional demands. Students bring a wide variety of challenges from home to your classroom. These are just a few of the things that make teaching hard. And it doesn't stop there: nationally, one in six teachers works a second job to make ends meet (National Center for Educational Statistics, 2018).

With this book, I would like to raise your expectations of what is possible in your classroom, from the very beginning of the year. Giving students the social and emotional skills they need early in the year can start a positive cycle where students feel a sense of connection with others in the classroom and work to keep that good feeling going. Taking the time for SEL when students feel calm is important. No one can learn new skills in the heat of the moment. Teaching students social and emotional skills and practicing those skills when students are relaxed and reflective means they will be able to use these skills when they need them. When students are working well together and seem to be in a groove, you will be less tired from managing difficult behavior and fixing so many problems after they occur.

What Are Social and Emotional Skills?

My hunch is that you have some sort of definition in your head about social and emotional skills. You are probably aware that none of us could actually make it through a morning without using these important skills. But what does this phrase really mean? For our purposes, we use this definition: Social and emotional learning refers to "the process through which children and adults understand and manage emotions, set and achieve positive goals, feel and show empathy for others, establish and maintain positive relationships, and make responsible decisions" (CASEL, 2019).

In this book, I focus on five social and emotional competencies described by the Collaborative for Academic, Social and Emotional Learning (CASEL, 2019). The following terms are adapted from those advanced by CASEL and enriched with ideas that promote equity based on work by Gregory and Fergus (2017).

- *Relationship skills* refer to the ability to create and sustain productive, healthy, positive relationships with people. These skills include communication, active listening, cooperation, resisting peer pressure, managing and negotiating conflict well, and offering and seeking help as needed. Developing relationship skills incorporates the ability to connect to others across differences in race, ethnicity, religion, age, disability, and social class.
- *Social awareness* is the ability to empathize with and take the perspective of other people from different backgrounds and cultures. It involves understanding norms for behavior and recognizing family, teachers, and people in the community as resources that can offer support. Becoming socially aware also means an awareness of others in terms of the ways their experiences have been shaped by systematic inequality in the U.S.
- *Self-management* refers to the ability to regulate one's emotions, thoughts, and behaviors effectively and in ways that match specific situations. This includes stress management, impulse control, self-motivation, and working toward personal and academic goals. When students or teachers experience a mismatch between their home and school cultures, self-management can take even more energy. In those cases, self-management involves code-switching, which means students (or adults) adjust their tone, language, or behavior to match the

immediate context so that members of the dominant cultural group feel comfortable.

- *Self-awareness* refers to one's ability to recognize and understand one's emotions and thoughts and the ways that these emotions influence behavior. Self-awareness involves the ability to size up one's strengths and limitations and links to a well-grounded sense of confidence and optimism. Self-awareness also includes an understanding of one's own identity (reflecting social class, race, religion, age) and understanding of some of the advantages or disadvantages that have been conferred automatically by society because of some aspects of that identity.

- *Effective decision making* means the ability to make productive choices about social interactions and personal behavior in ways that consider what is ethical, safe, socially realistic, and attuned to the well-being of self and others. Such decision making considers the consequences of actions as well.

All five of these skills were on display in the scenario at the start of this chapter. Students used relationship skills as they worked together in small groups. They exercised social awareness as they listened and incorporated ideas from the other students in their group and considered how their own actions changed the experience of others. They applied self-management skills to keep themselves motivated in the work and even accepted the disappointing news from their teacher that they could not rent a highway billboard to educate their whole city on the topic of single-use plastic. Students showed self-awareness as they let everyone in their group share their ideas instead of just talking nonstop and kept their frustration in check if things were not going as they had hoped. Students engaged in decision making as they identified problems, analyzed solutions, and worked on this project until the end.

Beyond the key skills that develop, the definition of social and emotional skills that we use focuses on how children and adults develop these skills. Children are constantly learning from the people around them. Implicit learning occurs when they watch adults in and outside their family, teachers, peers they admire, and people in media to learn social and emotional skills. Children are learning behavior all the time, but sometimes it is not the behavior that we want them to learn. I had a real wake-up call when I heard my then 2-year-old son use a four-letter word that started with "s" to express his anger. Children learn skills through explicit instruction, too. For example, when a teacher leads a lesson on emotions or how to speak respectfully, students learn those skills. When a teacher encourages a student to be self-confident in her work, the student becomes less dependent on others for affirmation.

One important idea here is that SEL refers to a process of learning. Your students are in the process of developing these skills, and your interactions with your students are critical in that development. All your conversations and interactions with students are multilayered. At the surface, the students are listening to the actual words that you are saying. Beneath the surface, students are discerning what you think of them and whether or not you respect them and take them seriously. As a part of this learning process, you are teaching students subtle social and emotional skills by the way that you look at them with care versus disdain, listen to them carefully versus dismissively, or treat them with the same level of importance and trust as others in your classroom.

We usually do not think about the ways that adults develop social and emotional skills, but this is a process too. Think about a time recently when you realized that something or someone was irritating you and then came up with a strategy so you would be less irritated in the situation. Nice job using your social and emotional skills. Consider a time when you navigated a sticky situation at work when a family wanted one thing for their child, but you and another teacher knew the child needed something different, and that led to a difficult conversation. Again, good work using these skills.

Engaging in SEL is a process for adults because adults are continuously developing people who encounter new situations that require novel approaches to address them. For instance, you may have an aging parent who is exhibiting a behavior she has never shown before. In coming up with the best response, you engage in the process of developing some new self-management and social skills. Perhaps you have a new school administrator at your school with a different style than anyone else with whom you have worked. Again, learning how to respond is a process—you will leverage skills you already have in hand and learn some new skills to apply to this situation. The key point here is that learning social and emotional skills is a developmental process that occurs over time and in interaction with the people around you.

WHAT DOES THE RESEARCH SAY?

Time spent on SEL can have valuable payoffs in academics and life beyond the classroom. A meta-analysis showed that use of SEL programs produced as much as an 11-percentile-point gain in achievement (Durlak, Weissberg, Dymnicki, Taylor, & Schellinger, 2011). These programs can also improve student achievement and social and emotional skills, even beyond the length of the program (from 6 months up to 18 years after receiving programs; Taylor, Oberle, Durlak, & Weissberg, 2017). Such long-term findings apply to students across different racial/ethnic and socioeconomic groups. It is the skills that matter. That means that students' actual social and emotional skills immediately after experiencing the SEL program appeared to forecast positive social behaviors and improved academic performance as well as less substance use, emotional distress, and conduct problems (Taylor et al., 2017). In other words, building students' social and emotional skills has positive short- and long-term payoff.

Let's Talk About Time

In my conversations with teachers, they often pose a tough question: "If I devote time to social and emotional learning, will this detract from time spent on academics?" That is an important question to ask. After 20 years of working with teachers, I find that the most common barrier to adopting new practices is time. I suggest two ways to think about this issue of time.

SEL Prevents Discipline Problems

Teaching social and emotional skills and conveying high expectations for children's behavior means that teachers spend less time managing problem behaviors and handling discipline issues. Keep in mind that students are always learning behaviors from the students around them. If those behaviors are destructive and demeaning, students will learn those behaviors. If those behaviors are prosocial and productive, students will learn those behaviors instead. By starting the year by explicitly teaching positive social and emotional skills, you are setting your students up for success. You are establishing a set of goals for your students and expecting them to operate at a high level of social competence. This can prevent many problems and challenges. You may be saving hours of discipline problems.

SEL Is Not Only What You Teach, but How You Teach

An SEL approach to teaching can take no extra instructional time in your classroom. Let SEL seep into the empty spaces of the classroom. Students will learn social and emotional skills from you if they feel that they know you and can trust you. Imagine that you are all waiting in line on the way to an all-school assembly. It is sort of empty time, right? The students are lined up, while you are monitoring and keeping an eye on your watch, and you have about 30 seconds when you are doing nothing but just waiting. You notice a student who has been challenging for you. You walk over and start a conversation—maybe you notice the football jersey he is wearing and start asking him about football. Perhaps you just talked to his mom, and you have something nice to say about the conversation. Maybe you noticed the topic of the book he chose from the library and start talking with him about it. In just a few seconds, you are relating to him and connecting—you are conveying that you care about him as a person and not just that you care that he learns to read or turns things in on time. By doing this, you are setting the stage for future SEL in that this student is much more likely to respond and learn from you because of the relationship and connection that he feels with you.

Here is another example. You are in the middle of a math lesson, and you need some whiteboard markers. You know the teacher in the next room over has some, and you would like to get them quickly so you can move forward on your lesson. You look over and see a student who is always on time, always responsible, and always listens to exactly what you say. You are very tempted to ask him to run across the hall and get those markers for you. But instead, you choose someone else. You choose the student who you think can do this, but it will be a little bit of a challenge for her. You know that there is a small chance that she will get distracted on the way, but you also know that she will feel special that you asked her to do this favor. You take a risk and call her up to talk with you. You lean down to her level and whisper in her ear, "Can you do me a big favor? We need the whiteboard markers from Mr. Stoll's class to move to our next lesson. Can you go get them and bring them back? I know you can do this without getting distracted or lost. What do you think? Okay—thanks." This exercise is so valuable—as beneficial as any kind of lesson you could give on self-control. You are exercising this child's ability to show self-control while also conveying a close relationship with the child (by leaning down to her level), telling her that she is special (by choosing her), and stating that you have high expectations for her behavior ("I know you can do this"). Chances are, you will get those markers.

I have a third example. Build SEL into your system of evaluation. As you teach various social and emotional skills in this book and beyond, build these skills into your regular academic rubrics. Ask students to complete self-evaluations of their work. For individual work, use questions like these: How much did you persevere in math this quarter? How resourceful were you on this social studies project? After group work, have the students in each group answer questions such as: Did we work well as a team? What percentage of the work did each person do on this project? Did everyone on this team get their ideas heard? Or simply: If this team worked together in the future, what could we do to improve? For older students, when you hand out rubrics before they complete an assignment, these assessments will give them one more way to think about how they engage in a project.

The Difference Between Goals and Strategies

The beginning of the year is a great time to establish goals for your classroom. These are general goals for your own use about what you hope and plan to do to improve SEL in your classroom this year. Here are some examples:

- I plan to create a classroom environment where every student knows that I care about them and have their best interest in mind.
- I will help students be kind and respectful to each other because children learn academics best when they can trust the people around them.
- I shall hold high, but realistic, expectations for students' behavior. Then, I will be patient and supportive as they step up to those expectations.
- I will create a classroom environment that is caring and warm and academically challenging.
- I will model the behavior that I want my students to learn.

Choose maybe three or four goals that you care about the most and want to strive for in this upcoming year. Make sure that the goals are big, broad-umbrella positive ideas that you can sustain throughout the year. Choose from among those recommended in this book or create your own. You may want to put these goals on your computer or phone as a background or pin them to a bulletin board or bathroom mirror at home. Hold these goals close at hand and let them remind you of your purpose and direction. On great days, these goals will remind you about basic principles of children's development, and they will help you keep your focus with this group of students. On rough days, these goals will help you see past the immediate chaos, annoyance, or stress and remind you of what is important.

Most importantly, let these goals guide you in choosing specific strategies, lessons, and teaching practices that you use in the classroom. Goals differ from strategies. Whereas goals are big-picture ideas, strategies are teaching practices that you use day-to-day to live out your goals. Strategies are the nuts-and-bolts actions. A metaphor may help here. Think of goals as your destination and the strategies as the modes of transportation that you use to get there.

> Stay oriented toward your goals all year long. Modify your strategies to achieve those goals to match the changing needs of your students, shifting demands at different times of the year, and your opinion on what is working or not.

Let us take this goal: Create a classroom environment where every student knows that I care about them and have their best interest in mind. Different strategies fit well with this goal. For instance, one strategy is that you may choose to stand at the door as your students are coming in each morning and greet them by name. In doing so, you notice their facial expressions and what seems to be on their mind. This improves the quality of your relationships with students and helps you be more attuned to the day-to-day ups and downs in their lives. Another strategy might be sending home notes or postcards that say, "You did well!" with students. When a student shines either academically or socially, you might write out what the child did in detail and send it home via mail, electronic means, or backpack to share this good news with the child's family.

Here is how the goals versus strategies apply to this book. This book provides a variety of strategies to help you develop social and emotional skills in your students. Each chapter offers a lesson on a specific topic that you can use with your classroom across one or several days. These chapters, created collaboratively with teachers, are chock full of ideas about how and why to teach these skills to students. Over three years, we tried out the lessons with teachers, received feedback from them, adjusted the lessons, tried them with a new group of teachers, and so on. The teachers we worked with ranged from rural to suburban and urban. We had teachers with racially/ethnically homogeneous classrooms—all white, all African American, or all Latinx. We had teachers with tremendous heterogeneity in terms of race, ethnicity, and English learner status. Virtually all the teachers with whom we worked had children with special needs in their classrooms, too.

That having been said, these lessons are just words on a page. They are a set of strategies that only come to life if they fit with your big-picture goals and you give them full effort in your classroom. They are simply tools that can be used. The real magic occurs when you have a big-picture goal in mind and you choose one of these lessons as a strategy to achieve your goal. So, that is to say, if you simply teach the lesson on active listening but you do not have clarity on why active listening is important in your classroom, then this lesson will fall completely flat. Likewise, if you do the active listening lesson and then forget to model active listening yourself, there is no way that this lesson will take off in your classroom. What I am recommending here is aligned action. That is, choose big-picture goals. Choose strategies that fit with your goals. Make those goals and strategies come alive in the classroom through both teaching and practice.

Keep in mind that the strategies in this book focus on the social and emotional aspects of the classroom. Of course, your role as a teacher encompasses academic learning. I raise this issue as an important reminder. I have seen classrooms that have lovely environments where teachers and students are socially attuned and connected with one another but there is little academic learning. Without high-quality, focused, intentional academic activities, students simply won't learn what they need to learn. Such classrooms do not set students up well for the future. As you're developing a couple SEL goals, I suggest you clarify your academic goals as well.

As you use these lessons, please use your good sense. Keep your goals in mind and adapt the strategies as needed so that they match both your goals and the needs of your classroom. You may need to use a book that is different from the one that I recommend or change some wording so that you feel ownership of the lessons in this book. You may need to adjust from a written to spoken activity to accommodate student needs in the classroom. To do this well, keep your focus on your goals but make adjustments to the strategies that you use to achieve these goals. You know your students best, and I trust you to take these lessons and make them work for your classroom of students.

Key Ideas to Teach SEL

One important idea in this book is that learning social and emotional skills involves acquiring small, specific skills that then can be combined into larger, more complex skills. The sequence of the lessons reflects this pattern. For instance, active listening and respectful communication come first in the sequence. Once students can listen actively and communicate respectfully, then they are ready for more advanced skills like respecting multiple perspectives, or giving and receiving feedback. Likewise, managing frustration and anger come early in the sequence. After students have learned to be aware of these emotional states and have developed a range of skills to manage those strong emotions, students are capable of learning about perseverance and then developing skills to resolve conflict.

Yet another premise of this book is the idea that we have limited cognitive capacity as humans. Break SEL into small baby steps. In Chapter 2 on respectful communication, I talk about teaching sentence stems such as, "I agree with you because . . . " Learning a new skill like using sentence stems in conversation draws from students' cognitive resources. So it is best to start using sentence stems on simple examples that do not introduce unfamiliar academic content and do not carry a lot of emotion. In other words, when teaching students to use sentence stems to disagree, use noncontroversial content. Choose a simple topic (e.g., "Which tastes better—pears or apples?") instead of something very complex ("Which is a better way to do this problem—addition or multiplication?") or something that may elicit very strong opinions ("Which is the better team, the Lakers or the Bulls?").

You will notice that all the lessons in this book share a few common features. To start, there are activities or questions to elicit students' prior knowledge of a topic. Then the lesson offers instruction involving trade books and/or discussion to teach, model, discuss, and explore new skills. Next, the lessons offer students an opportunity to practice skills either in writing or in paired discussion to consolidate their learning. Finally, there are activities designed to help students apply the newly learned skills to instructional activities, different settings, and new situations. After these lessons, teachers play an important role in letting these ideas flourish in the classroom by reminding students to use their new skills.

To use these lessons, it helps to have a pad of chart paper and markers. Then you can post the anchor charts on the walls of your classroom and refer to what you have written there. Many of the trade books we recommend are available to purchase. If needed, video versions of many of these books are available on the web. If you choose a video version, please be engaged and discuss these books much as you would do for a read-aloud to unpack the wealth of ideas about social and emotional competence.

A final point has to do with timing. Start teaching these skills early in the year, if possible, then use follow-up and support throughout the year. Time spent orienting students to these skills in August, September, and October means that they will become integrated into students' routine behavior. Yes, it will be crucial for you to offer occasional reminders and some redirection; but you will not be starting from scratch midway through the year if you used SEL from the start.

SEL From the Start

Develop Classroom Norms

We walked into a fourth-grade classroom when the students were getting ready to do a math project on estimation. Students were going to a small nearby park to estimate how many squirrels were in the whole park. The teacher assigned students to groups of three or four and gave them maps of the park, each with an assigned region indicated. The teacher led the students to the park and asked each group to sit in their region and count the squirrels they saw in that segment during a 10-minute period. Then students came back to the classroom and exchanged information among groups. Next, each small group estimated how many squirrels were in the whole park and then discussed and wrote down reasons their estimates might be too high or too low.

Success with this math activity completely depends on the classroom culture. Will students work with each other on the task? Will students find the location that corresponds to their segment on the map? Will students actually sit in the park in their assigned location, count the squirrels, and write the information down as expected? Will students come back into the classroom and share their answers with the other groups? This activity exercises many social and emotional skills. Students need to exhibit self-control on the way to the park. They need relationship skills and social awareness to work with one another and tune into the strengths of members in their group so they can find the right place to sit and determine the parameters of their region of the park. The talented teacher leading this exercise had established classroom norms in the beginning of the year. She had discussed how all of the students wanted their classroom to look, sound, and feel. In morning circle before engaging in this activity, she discussed their classroom norms: Be Responsible; Be Caring; Be Safe; Be Respectful. She asked the students to name specific behaviors they would need to carry out this activity in a way that matched these norms. The students' responses showed that this activity was within reach and that the group work would enhance, not detract from, the point of the lesson. It is clear that the teacher and students had taken time in the beginning of the year to establish classroom norms and that these norms were setting the stage for student-centered instruction. Kudos to this teacher for creating a sense of community and close relationships in the classroom. Let's talk about classroom norms as a way to jump-start your efforts to create a positive classroom culture.

What Are Classroom Norms?

Classroom norms are a set of positive guidelines for how teachers and students work together in a classroom. These norms create a shared culture that plays out in the way that teachers and students talk with each other and how students interact. Classroom norms establish high and positive expectations for student behavior. As students live these norms, they practice self-awareness and self-management by noticing the way that their own behaviors fit with classroom expectations and then adjust their behavior to match those expectations. Students practice social awareness and relationship skills by recognizing the needs of others and operating in a way that allows everyone to learn in their classroom. Students engage in effective decision making as they make choices that show that they understand the consequences of their actions.

As a teacher, you probably have an astute sense of how norms play out in school environments. Think about your last staff meeting. Did you go to the meeting with an air of excitement and curiosity or maybe a bit of dread? Did you attend knowing that you would learn something new or did you get that low, humdrum feeling that comes from hearing the same old thing over and over again? Did you walk into the room knowing that your opinions would be respected as much as other people's or did you start the meeting with the notion that some teachers' views would be privileged more than others? The staff at your school have a set of norms for behavior. At most schools, the norms are not established explicitly. That means that there is no conversation among the adults about how to interact. Still, an implicit culture develops and plays out. That implicit culture may be inspiring and exciting, or it may be negative, frustrating, and even toxic. Whether we like it or not, more experienced faculty at your school tend to teach that culture to the new teachers with comments like, "You'll be pleasantly surprised. This is a supportive place to be, and the teachers are team players here," or "These meetings are just a waste of our time."

The point here is that all social groups have a set of norms that guide behavior. Most often, these norms evolve implicitly. Implicit norms may be terrific or not so great. However, classroom norms are so important that it is better not to leave them up to chance. Think *Lord of the Flies*. In your class-room, you can work with your students to create norms for how they want their learning environment to be. Students will buy into these norms if they play an active role in creating them and carrying them out. As students create and live by positive norms, you will see a culture emerge that is trusting and caring, which then brings out the best in your students.

Take time in the beginning of the year to create classroom norms. Although it takes precious time, these norms can be a gift that keeps on giving all year long. Behavior is contagious, and positive behavior leads to pleasant, smiling, comfortable kids, whereas negative behavior leads to kids who blame, tease, and annoy one another. Throughout the year, it is crucial to keep norms active. You can refer back to them and even revise them, if needed. As a teacher, it's important that you model these norms in your own behaviors. Students can give each other gentle reminders too. These norms are like the foundation of a house, and, if developed well, you will prevent sloping floors and expensive repairs.

WHAT DOES THE RESEARCH SAY?

Classroom norms strengthen relationships—both between teachers and students and among students themselves. High-quality, authentic, and positive relationships make a tremendous difference for student learning. By definition, high-quality teacher-student relationships are low in conflict and high in closeness and support. Research on elementary school students shows that high-quality relationships contribute to students' resiliency and academic performance (Curby, Rimm-Kaufman, & Ponitz, 2009; Hamre & Pianta, 2005; McCormick & O'Connor, 2015; Rudasill, Reio, Stipanovic, & Taylor, 2010).

The quality of peer relationships matters, as well. Children who are excluded by peers in the early elementary school years are less likely to participate in class and show lower achievement in the later elementary school years. Statistical techniques used to explain this finding revealed that being excluded and abused by peers (e.g., kids saying bad things about them) leads to poor achievement (Buhs, Ladd, & Herald, 2006). Teachers matter. Demonstrate that you like all the children in the class, signal that everyone in the class is valuable, contradict students when they show prejudice toward another child, and reduce the sense of haves and have nots in the classroom. These teacher behaviors improve positive interactions among students (Mikami, Lerner, & Lun, 2010).

Establish Classroom Norms

Generate Excitement About the Learning Ahead

Start your conversation about establishing classroom norms by generating excitement about the year ahead. Talk about some of the interesting academic work that the class will be doing. Explain how students will be working with others in their classroom. Describe some cool books that you will be reading and discussing. Dig into details about the new math games, manipulatives, or computer activities that will be part of your instruction. Tell your students about the exciting year of learning that lies ahead. Then explain that you want their help in creating the kind of classroom environment that makes it easy for great work to happen.

Introduce Classroom Norms

Talk about classroom norms. Ask students about what they think the word "norms" means. Define norms as a set of guidelines for how we work together in our classroom. Explain that you will be working with them to create the classroom norms that you will follow all year long.

Generate Student Ideas on How the Classroom Should Look, Sound, and Feel

Next, raise the question, "How do you want our classroom to look, sound, and feel for great work to happen?" Students will chime in with ideas like "sound quiet," "feel welcoming," and similar phrases. Asking this question gets student to think about what it feels like to be in an environment where they feel calm, trusted, and comfortable trusting others.

Ask Students About Behavior That Will Create This Ideal Classroom

Prompt them further with the question, "What would normal behavior look like if we were all doing our best work and supporting others to do their best, too?" Most likely, your students will start peppering you with statements phrased in the negative like, "Don't be angry," "Don't be super loud," and "Don't be mean." You can help students reword their ideas in the positive and write these ideas on a whiteboard or a couple pieces of chart paper.

You can use two different markers here. Use one color to record what students say about how the class should look, sound, and feel and another color for students' ideas about behaviors that they may need to show to create a classroom that looks, sounds, and feels a certain way. Use language that will be clear for all the students in your classroom, including English learners, if possible.

Create Broad Categories and Identify Example Behaviors

Now that you have all these ideas on a big whiteboard or chart paper, the next step is to have your students work with you to create broad categories. For upper elementary school students, ask students to help you figure out which ones relate to each other. Use student responses about how they want their classroom to look, sound, and feel. Then create broad categories based on student ideas. Likewise, use student responses about behaviors they will need to show. Ideally, we want students to come up with broad categories and behaviors because it engages them more deeply in the process. For younger children, you will need to provide some extra support to generate the broad categories. First, identify the broad categories yourself and then encourage students to sort the ideas they generated under these broad categories. For instance, as you discuss behaviors, you can say, "I am noticing that many of the behaviors that you have brainstormed fall under the category of respect. Who can come to the board and show a behavior that demonstrates being respectful?" After a few examples like this, the students may be able work together to try to identify broad categories for the remaining behaviors on the board.

Obviously, it would be easier for you to do this alone. But the point of engaging your students in this process is that it gets students thinking deeply about how they want their classroom to look, sound and feel, as well as the specific behaviors needed to uphold the norms of their classroom. Also, as an extra bonus, this process expands their vocabulary of positive behaviors.

Some teachers choose to create norms in just one or two days during the first week of school, either in one sitting or multiple sittings. Other teachers, particularly in the younger grades, spread this conversation over a few days or a week of class. The advantage of doing this all on the first couple days of school is that the norms will be in place quickly. The advantage of rolling this lesson out slowly is that you distribute the process over many days, which means shorter sessions each time so students do not get bored. Also, a gradual process can help these norms stick. Either of these approaches works, so choose the one that seems to work for you and your students.

As students start generating broad categories, stop occasionally to get feedback from the full group on how they feel about living with these norms. For instance, when students generate, "Be Respectful," ask your students for their opinion on whether they thought this phrase was a good fit with a lot of their ideas. Ask students to show what they think with their thumbs. For instance, say, "What do you think about the phrase, 'Be Respectful'? Does that work for you as a classroom norm? If yes, give me a thumbs up; if no, give me a thumbs down; and if you can live with it, thumbs to the side."

Introduce the Idea of Consensus

This is a great time to introduce the idea of consensus, which you can use later in your classroom to reinforce a collaborative classroom climate. A consensus is an agreement or decision that everyone in the group can support. Point out that a consensus is reached when everyone responds to an idea with either thumbs up or thumbs to the side. By introducing the idea of consensus to students early in the year, you give them language they can use in their small-group interactions. It can be exciting to hear a third grader explain to you that she and her partner came to a consensus on a decision.

Now, let's be realistic. You know your students well, and pushing for consensus may simply not work in a classroom where you have a few students who enjoy being naysayers. In that case, you may spend too much time working toward a consensus, and you could lose the point of the lesson. If you have this concern in your classroom, you may want to introduce the phrase "majority decision," which can be equally valuable in the future.

Write the Norms on Chart Paper or a Whiteboard

Next, keep working with your students to consolidate the broad categories, identify example behaviors and make a final version. (Figure 1.1) First, list how the class decided they wanted their classroom to look, sound, and feel. For instance, "Our classroom environment should look organized, sound fair and feel welcoming and fun . . ." Then list behaviors needed to create a classroom environment like this. For example, in our classroom we should be "responsible, caring, safe, and respectful." You can list student-generated behaviors that go with these broad categories. For instance, under "Be Responsible," you might list specific examples including, "Take care of supplies," "Be helpful," "Do your best," and "Stay focused." When you list specific behavioral examples, students see their own ideas incorporated into the final product. They serve as a good reminder.

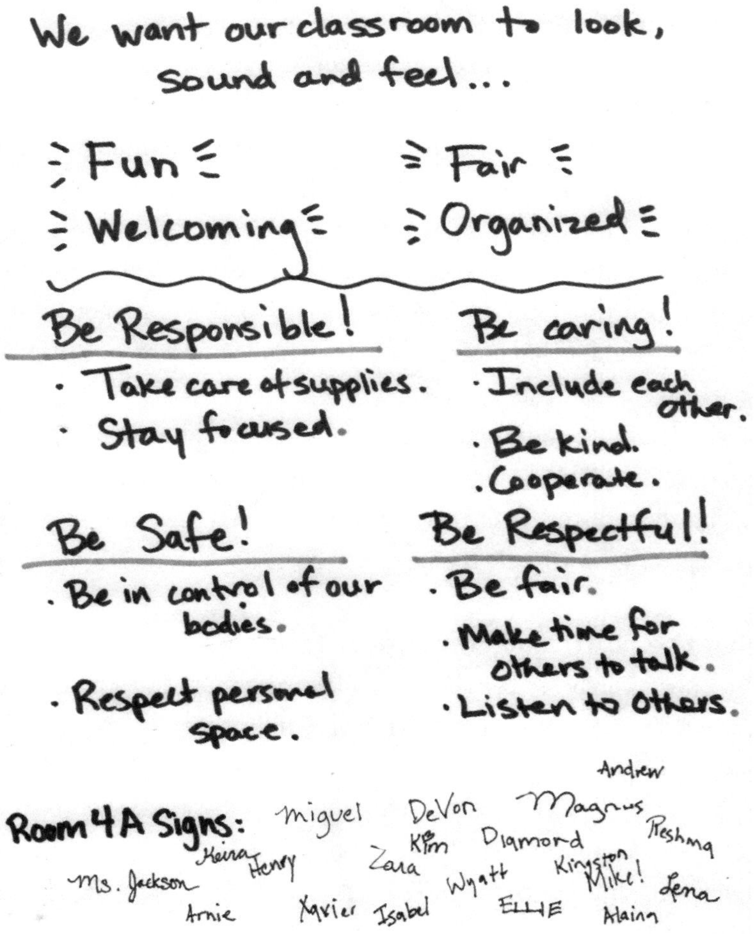

We want our classroom to look, sound and feel...

≥ Fun ≤   ≥ Fair ≤

≥ Welcoming≤   ≥ Organized ≤

Be Responsible!
- Take care of supplies.
- Stay focused.

Be Caring!
- Include each other.
- Be kind.
- Cooperate.

Be Safe!
- Be in control of our bodies.
- Respect personal space.

Be Respectful!
- Be fair.
- Make time for others to talk.
- Listen to others.

Room 4A Signs: miguel DeVon Magnus Andrew Reshma
Ms. Jackson Keira Henry Kim Diamond Kingston Lena
Arnie Xavier Isabel Zara Wyatt ELLIE Mike! Alaina

FIGURE 1.1. This is an example of a completed set of classroom norms.

Confirm Buy-In From Students

After this process of creating the norms, it is time to revisit whether everyone in the class can live with them. Remind students that it is important that you all come up with norms that you can all agree upon and support. Revisit the idea of consensus. Look at the final set of classroom norms and ask students to indicate thumbs up, thumbs down, or thumbs sideways. Do some working and reworking until everyone is at thumbs up or thumbs sideways. Then ask your students to sign the paper to demonstrate their willingness to adopt the norms. Hang the chart in an obvious place in the classroom at the students' eye level.

The work to this point may seem like a colossal effort. But, spread over several days, it will be easier than it seems. After completing this chart, it is important to help students feel a sense of pride and accomplishment in the norms. Celebrate with a class game or a cheer.

Revisit the Norms as Needed

Keeping norms active is a challenging yet important task. Sadly, we have all seen an aged poster with classroom norms hanging by one last pin, partially covered by other student work, resting inactively as it approaches the end of its life cycle in the recycling bin. It takes active work to keep norms as a part of classroom life.

One way to keep norms animated is by referring to them regularly throughout the day. One fourth grade teacher had a particularly talkative group of students and often revisited their norm "Everyone's voice should be heard in our classroom" to remind some students to talk less so others could chime in. In future days and weeks, discuss the norms with your students and practice them. Before transitioning between activities, talk about how students can make the transition in a responsible, caring, safe, and respectful way. Discuss the specific behaviors needed, then make the transition and reflect on ways that your collective behavior matched these norms. Let norms be a dynamic and growing part of the culture, not a stagnant feature of the classroom. When a new challenging situation arises, look at your students with interest and say, "You know, we don't have a norm that addresses this concern. Let's make one."

Norms are shared by everyone in the classroom community. Students can gently nudge other students to remember their classroom norms. Pair students and have them practice using respectful language to remind each other of the norms. The explicit practice is important because otherwise students may use norms as an opportunity to tease. With practice, one student may say to another, "Remember that one of our norms is to be organized. Do you want me to help you with your stuff on the floor?" As an adult, you can model these norms by having a conversation with a student or another teacher and pointing out how the way you talked fits with your classroom norms.

Reflect on the Norms

In future days and weeks, reflect on your norms. Discuss what aspects of the norms are easy or difficult to follow. Remind students of the norms when they meet expectations as well as when they fall short. Talk about situations that make it difficult to follow the norms and listen to what your students say at face value. This process can help you understand what situations are most challenging to your students, and then you can make small adjustments to how you organize those situations.

Create natural extensions of these classroom norms, especially with upper elementary students. Keep in mind that you are supporting their development of self-understanding and self-management, and that it is critical for students to develop these skills before they launch into their middle school years. You can set up opportunities for students to write (or draw) privately about these norms toward the beginning of the year. One question set per day can be a great way to start each school day. Here are three sets of example questions.

Question Set 1 helps students think about their own strengths and weaknesses in self-management.

- Which norms do you think will be easiest for you to follow? Why?
- Which norms do you think will be hardest for you to follow? Why?

Question Set 2 helps students become aware of how their self-control varies depending on the time of day or activities available to them.

- Are there some times in the day when it is hard to follow classroom norms? What times and why?
- Are there certain places in the classroom where it is hard to follow classroom norms?
- What places and why?

Question Set 3 helps students become self-aware of their behavior in social situations. These questions develop ideas and skills needed to resist peer pressure. Because students may generate examples about specific students in their classroom, it is especially important that these answers are not discussed aloud.

- Think about the other students in your classroom. Is it hard to follow the norms when you work with some people compared to others?
- Think about your close friends in the classroom. Is it easy or hard to keep the classroom norms when you work with your close friends? What makes it easy or hard?

Build the Norms Into Daily Life

There are a few other variations and extensions that can support a positive classroom culture and consolidate student buy-in to the norms. For instance, have a conversation about how the culture of the classroom can vary from day to day. Point out that the class cannot be perfect with its norms. Remind students that the norms are there to help create the kind of classroom where great learning can happen but that we will make mistakes along the way. Help students understand that making mistakes with norms is like making mistakes in reading or math. If we are not making mistakes, then we are probably not setting high enough goals for ourselves, which means we are probably not learning.

For group projects, use the norms to create a self-assessment tool (e.g., checklist). Small groups can use the checklist to rate how they did at following the norms during an activity. After students finish their group work, they can reflect on each norm and decide whether they did a good job living by that norm or whether they need more work. If they rate their success low, they can generate a strategy to do better next time. For instance, if a norm is, "We want our classroom to feel respectful, fair, and caring," and students rate themselves as low on this norm because people keep interrupting each other, they could introduce the classroom equivalent of the Native American talking stick. Each person needs to hold the stick in order to talk. Then they make sure that everyone has had a chance to hold the talking stick. Alternatively, they could decide that when they come up with something to discuss, they make sure that everyone states their opinion (or says "pass") before moving on to the next topic.

Norms can be complicated for students new to English and/or unfamiliar with school life in the U.S. Use visual representations that show examples of student behavior that match the classroom norms. Michelle Katz, a teacher with all English learners, helped students create and understand categories for their norms by printing out pictures of students helping each other, cleaning up after themselves, and sharing with classmates. She asked the students to match the pictures to the categories of norms as a way of deepening their understanding of desired behaviors in the classroom. By using pictures of the students in these visual representations, the students felt personally connected to the norms of helping each other, being organized, and being safe.

STEPS FOR CREATING CLASSROOM NORMS

1. Get students excited about the learning ahead.

2. Introduce the idea of establishing classroom norms as a way of deciding how they want their classroom to look, sound, and feel for learning to be interesting and fun.

3. Ask students to generate ideas for how they want their classroom to look, sound, and feel for great work to happen. Ask students about the behaviors they need to show to create a classroom that looks, sounds, and feels the way they want it to be. Help students reword their ideas as positive statements and write the student ideas on a whiteboard or chart paper.

5. Create groupings and broad categories. Work with students to use their ideas to create 3–4 broad categories to describe how their classroom should look, sound, and feel. Next, work with students to identify behaviors needed to create a classroom environment that looks, sounds, and feels the way they want it to be. Build buy-in from your students as you do this.

6. Introduce the idea of consensus.

7. Write the norms on chart paper or a whiteboard. First list how the class decided they wanted their classroom to look, sound, and feel. Then list behaviors needed to create a classroom environment like this.

8. Confirm buy-in from students. Invite the students to sign the paper to demonstrate their adoption of the norms.

9. Revisit the norms as needed. Keep them active in your classroom.

10. Reflect on what norms are easy or hard to follow. Reflect on when it might be easy or difficult to follow them. Follow up individually with students who have behavioral needs if they struggle with the norms.

11. Build the norms into daily life. Refer back to the norms to remind students about the classroom culture that makes learning productive and fun.

Summary: Why Create Norms?

Establishing classroom norms offers an approach to creating a classroom culture with great intention and collaboration with students. Students will learn and internalize positive social behaviors through the day-to-day practice of those norms, which can become shorthand reminders of teachers' high expectations for behavior. Norms such as "Let everyone be true to who they are" and "We are all equally important in this class" can set the stage for valuing cultural differences among students and creating a less hierarchical classroom. Discussion of the norms can help teachers understand what their students find easy or difficult to do.

The idea of creating classroom rules is certainly not new for most teachers, but the idea of norms may bring a new twist (Denton & Kriete, 2000).

Norms refer to typical social behavior, whereas rules describe a set of regulations to guide behavior. Norms sound optimistic and positive ("Imagine what you'd like your classroom to be like and feel like"), whereas rules seem more punitive ("Follow these rules or harsh punishments may follow.") We recommend creating norms instead of rules in your classroom. But if you prefer rules, go for it. The goal here is to establish expectations for behavior and create a culture of caring where students feel safe, supported, and comfortable taking academic risks.

One fourth grade teacher we talked to used norms and noticed that students were more respectful and kind to one another and that her classroom ran more smoothly. As one example, the students in her classroom were protective and accepting of a girl with extreme autism. One child had "a particularly difficult personality." The teacher noticed that the other students were kind to her and didn't bully her. Creating a positive classroom culture naturally brings out opportunities for students to practice and model kindness, acceptance, fairness, empathy, patience, and other important skills.

Let us return to the math estimation task at the beginning of this chapter. Most teachers would read through a lesson like that and think there was no way that they could pull it off in a 50-minute math period. Disaster would ensue. This teacher and her students began their school year by establishing norms and had been working on developing a positive classroom culture for months. Now they got to reap the benefits of that work. They were easily able to apply their norms to a new activity and pull off a very complex lesson with respect and efficiency. Not only that, but the students got to experience an authentic estimation activity, enjoy a chance to go outside during math class, shine new light on their urban environment, and work together toward a common classroom goal.

Teach Active Listening

It was Jasmine's turn to share in her first-grade classroom's morning circle. The previous day, she had lost her first tooth, and she brought it to class in a little white envelope to show it to everyone. She was bursting with excitement. After just a few sentences about where she lost it, how much it hurt, and how much she got from the tooth fairy, she opened the conversation up for questions. The students were very excited to talk—they raised their hands, waved their arms around vigorously, and squirmed and wiggled with enthusiasm. When Jasmine called on the students, they talked about their own teeth—one child had three that were loose, another swallowed a tooth once, and yet another got his knocked out by his brother. The class had a discussion about teeth for a few minutes, and the teacher moved on to the next student. But did Jasmine get a true conversation about her experience losing her tooth? Not really. The students barely listened. All they actually heard was the word "tooth" before they launched into their own thoughts about their own dental experiences.

We've all had situations where students hardly listen to one another or hurry along a friend so they can blurt out what they want to say. Imagine how different your classroom would be if students slowed down and really listened to what others say. Active listening is an act of caring and kindness. It is a skill that can be taught and practiced. Over time, your students will be able to use this and apply it to actual lessons in the classroom.

What Is Active Listening?

Active listening is a kind of communication in which a person pays attention to a conversational partner so well that, if asked, the person could repeat what the speaker is saying. It means not just listening to the words, but also hearing the meaning and intent behind them. Successful active listening involves social awareness in that students need to take the perspective of and empathize with others. Active listening is a critical ability for developing relationship skills, including clear communication, cooperation, and successful negotiation of conflict.

As an adult, it's worth taking a moment to think about the extent to which the people around you use active listening in conversations you've had. Think about those people who listen carefully to what you say and reflect deeply on your words and ideas. They ask you what you mean. They seem to want to understand your life, not just talk about their own. Think about a time you've called an old friend and you hear him reflect and build upon what you've said. How did that make you feel? Did you feel understood? Cared for? Did you feel like what you said matters?

Let's contrast that with other conversations you've had. Perhaps you've been in a staff meeting where people are interrupting each other. Although everyone is talking, people's sentences seem disconnected from one another and show no sense of coherence. That might be fine if it's a brainstorming session, but if the purpose is to work together to solve a problem, these behaviors show little caring and connection. This approach to communication is unlikely to steer toward a solution. Active listening is a very basic skill, yet we see many instances where it's not used by the kids and adults around us. We see this in politics, for example. Slowing down and listening sets the stage for positive, caring relationships. Active listening is a critical first step to enable people to see each other's perspective and work together with others who are different from themselves to produce solutions to problems.

WHAT DOES THE RESEARCH SAY?

Do children understand what it means to listen? A classic study by McDevitt, Spivey, Sheehan, Lennon, and Story (1990) examines children's ideas of what it means to be a good listener when someone is talking. The researchers asked first, third, and fifth graders what good listeners do and do not do. First graders emphasized the behaviors needed to listen carefully. They talked about turning their attention to the person talking and being nondisruptive (not playing with their pencils, for example). Third and fifth graders also mentioned the behavioral aspects of listening, but these older children also emphasized the psychology behind active listening. Specifically, third and fifth graders said that good listeners make active efforts to comprehend the other person including "learning from what they heard" and "knowing what's happening." These findings suggest that third and fifth graders know that it takes work to understand what someone is saying.

Active listening requires a range of skills. Students need to focus their attention on the speaker, process the language heard, and retain information, which involves working memory. Existing research shows that teachers can change students' understanding of what it means to listen well so that even young children understand that it takes work and effort to understand another person who is talking (Crosskey & Vance, 2011).

Teaching Active Listening

To teach active listening, we recommend that you start by modeling it. Bring in a helpful assistant—another adult or a student in your class. You can choose a specialist at your school who may have a few minutes or have your principal visit to engage in this exercise. Alternatively, choose a student who tends to get a bit less attention in class so that your students get practice in listening to someone who is often sidelined in conversations. Ask your students to watch you as you model the behavior and tell them to notice how you act.

Ask your helpful assistant to choose an experience to tell the class. It might be about a time when they fell off a bicycle, a time when they went on a new roller coaster or an activity that they did with people in their family. If you've asked a child to be your helpful partner, you may want to ask them about their topic in a private conversation before modeling this to the class. As you know, some conversations about families are "private share" topics—not something you would like a student to share with the group.

Model a Conversation

Tell your class that you are going to model what active listening looks like. Suggest to your students that they should watch you very carefully and notice how you act. Then ask your helpful assistant to tell you a story. As you listen, make eye contact with the person talking, face the person, and nod to acknowledge what the other person is saying. Wait until your helpful assistant has completely stopped talking and then ask a follow-up question.

Ask your students to describe what active listening looks like. Ask them, "What did you notice about my body language? What were my eyes doing?

What did you notice about my mouth? And what do you think was going on in my mind?" Ask them to think about what you might be feeling while you listen. Affirm your students' responses when they say that you're watching the person who is talking, showing attention, and listening in a way that shows you're thinking about your partner.

Create a Visual Representation

It can be helpful to make active listening behaviors even more concrete by asking the students to help you fill out a diagram of a person. Here are some questions and target responses to consider:

- When you're listening actively, what are your eyes doing? (Watching and looking at the person talking.)
- What are your ears doing? (Both ears are ready to hear.)
- What is your mouth doing? (It's closed and quiet.)
- What is your brain doing? (Thinking about what is being said.)
- What is your heart doing? (Caring about what the other person is saying.)

The figures here can be projected onto a whiteboard, printed out, or drawn onto easel chart paper. The teachers we worked with, who mostly taught students of color, liked Figure 2.1 because it looked like their students. With this figure, you can add labels as you go. Figure 2.2 is a similar figure of a white boy with the labels already on it.

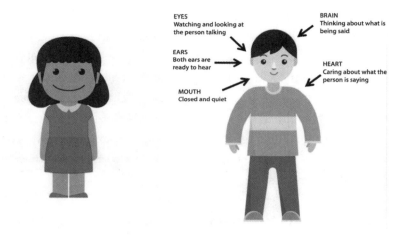

FIGURE 2.1 (*left*). Use this image to help teach active listening if you want to add the labels as you go.

FIGURE 2.2 (*right*). This is an alternative image for teaching active listening with labels already added.

Some people may choose to give the picture a name (e.g., Hannah Hears or Logan the Listener). Keep in mind that you will be referring back to this anchor chart throughout the lesson and school year.

Teach About Paraphrasing

Next, introduce the concept of paraphrasing and demonstrate how good active listening means that you can paraphrase your partner's ideas. "When we paraphrase what someone else said, we are restating their ideas and thoughts in our own words. This means we are thinking carefully about what the other person is saying, not generating our own thoughts and ideas while we listen. Listening this carefully is a sign that we care about the person who is talking and understand what they said." Remind your students of why we listen—we want our partners to feel heard and respected. Work together to paraphrase the story told by your helpful assistant. After hearing input from your students, see if you can give a paraphrased version of your assistant's story in just a couple of sentences. Do so in a way that shows that you've heard and respected your partner.

Have Students Model and Practice Active Listening

Now it is time to ask two students to model active listening and paraphrasing. Call on two students and assign one to be the speaker and the other to be the listener. To manage the scope here, suggest a topic that is interesting but not too interesting. If the students start talking about their last birthday party or sports at the end of a championship season, the activity can quickly get out of hand and derail the lesson. Instead, suggest a favorite school subject or recess activity. (You know your students best—choose accordingly.) Ask the speaker to talk about the topic and the listener to demonstrate their active listening abilities. After the pair of students model the behavior, ask the rest of the class to share what they noticed about the model pair. Repeat the students' responses and show how they correspond to your anchor chart to support learning. Ask your students to notice features of paraphrasing and what worked and didn't work.

Pair Students to Practice Active Listening

After you're comfortable that your students understand the correspondence between the behaviors they see and those represented on the anchor chart, invite all students to choose a partner with whom to practice active listening and paraphrasing. Remind your students to choose short anecdotes, not breakfast-to-bed stories that go on and on. Organize the time so each student gets a chance to listen and paraphrase someone's idea and speak and have their own idea paraphrased. Circulate to make sure each partner gets a chance to talk and be the active listener.

Reflect as a Group

At last, you are ready for one of the most important parts of this experience. It is time to consolidate your students' learning. Ask your students a few questions to reflect on their experiences. You can do this as a large group, ask students to reflect with their already established partners, ask students to get into groups of four for reflection, or give students an opportunity to respond in writing. How you do this is up to you. What's important here is that you don't skimp on the opportunity to reflect.

Here are a few questions to ask:

- What did your partner do with their body that showed that they were listening to you?
- How did it feel to be listened to?

- What was it like when someone paraphrased your ideas?
- How did it feel to be a listener? Was it hard or easy? Was it hard or easy to paraphrase?
- When do you think it would be a good idea to use active listening?
- How did active listening feel similar to and different from how you usually listen?

Remind Students to Use Their Active Listening Skills in Upcoming Instruction

Close the lesson by linking active listening to other experiences that students will have in the classroom. For instance, you might remind them that in science class, they do a lot of activities that require talking about scientific ideas. Mention that they can use their active listening skills in science. Mention the books that you're reading together as a class. You can remind them that when they are listening actively, their conversations can get a lot better and more interesting. If you have a guest coming to class in the next few days or weeks, you can tell students that they will need their active listening skills in these situations, too.

STEPS FOR TEACHING ACTIVE LISTENING

1. Model a conversation. Discuss how you and your partner showed active listening.

2. Use an anchor chart of a person to show what the ears, mouth, and eyes are doing while listening actively.
3. Introduce the idea of paraphrasing.
4. Ask two students to model active listening and paraphrasing to the class.
5. Reflect on the students' success.
6. Pair students to practice active listening while you monitor.
7. Reflect as a group.
8. Remind students to use their active listening skills in upcoming days, weeks, and months as you teach academic content involving student conversation.

Summary: Why Teach Active Listening?

Spending this much time to learn active listening may feel unproductive and slow. But this skill is foundational to successful, caring relationships in the classroom. Once students have mastered this skill and know it by name, you have an incredible new tool to use in the future. Invoking active listening helps your students slow down and think deeply, and this is where the learning occurs.

As a skilled teacher, you will probably notice ways that you can design this lesson artfully to amplify the voices of students who are not often heard. As you watch students practicing their active listening, notice the most introverted students in your class and consider what it is like for them to have their own ideas repeated back to them. Consider the experience from the perspective of English learners, especially those who may be aware of their language accents—what is it like for them to hear their ideas spoken by a native English–speaking peer? For shy students or those new to English, it can be very empowering for them to hear their own ideas said by another person.

It almost goes without saying that active listening can support self-control for the big talkers in your classroom. For some students, listening like this may be an entirely new experience. Very young students who have difficulty with self-control may find it helpful to put their hands over their mouth while their partner is speaking. This little physical act reminds them whose turn it is to talk. Older students will need to focus and direct their attention carefully so they are tuned into the person talking and not thinking about their own ideas. You can notice which students are able to master active listening and which ones seem to have trouble. In one-on-one conversations, you can model your active listening as a student is conferencing with you or retelling a story from the playground or home. Be explicit with the student: "Notice I'm doing active listening here . . ." to reinforce the concept.

Let's go back to Jasmine from the beginning of this chapter. Imagine that Jasmine shared her good news about her tooth, and the students in her class asked her questions about it. They asked, "When did you lose your tooth?" "Did it hurt?" "Was there a lot of blood?" "Did the tooth fairy come, and what did you get?" In doing so, the students in the class are affirming

Jasmine's personal experience and making her feel noticed and important. The students who listen to Jasmine create a bridge for Jasmine between what happened at home and what is occurring in school. For those few minutes in the class, Jasmine feels heard. She feels like she matters and what happened to her is important. This small act of kindness gives Jasmine a little sense of agency—when she takes a little action in her own world, the world responds to her action. In that moment, she matters. Using active listening can create many moments that matter for children. These moments plant seeds of initiative and support the development of social skills in the classroom and beyond.

Respectful
Communication

I visited an English language arts class. The lesson was over with about eight minutes left in the class. The teacher put three words on the board: there, they're, and their. She called one student to the board at a time and asked the student to point to which word she was using in a sentence. Her sentences were funny. They were based on her own personal (but not too personal) life and made the students laugh. She said, "After school, I went down the street and saw my neighbors walking their three dogs and holding their little poop bags." The student at the board pointed to "their." The teacher asked the other students, "Do all of you agree?" There was hustle and bustle. Most students agreed but one student responded, "Let's see. I hear your point but I don't agree. It's T-H-E-R-E!" The teacher asked him why he thought his answer was correct. The student explained his answer (albeit incorrect). A few other students chimed in, and they came up with the correct solution as a class.

In listening to this conversation, it was easy to notice that the student who disagreed said, "I hear your point." In doing so, he showed respect for the student who had taken a bit of a risk by going up to the board to answer the question. I watched the class laughing and making a game out of this activity, and I noticed a pattern. All the students were using respectful language as they agreed and disagreed with one another. A conversation with the teacher after the class revealed the explanation. Not only did she work with the class to develop norms to create a positive classroom climate, but she explicitly taught respectful communication language to the students and encouraged them to practice it. In this example, the question asked had one right answer. Their respectful communication with one another served to strengthen the relationships among the students. For other conversations in this class, such as when students were drawing inferences from a text, these respectful communication skills were crucial for healthy disagreement and deep conversations about the reading that they had done.

What Is Respectful Communication?

Respectful communication is a way of speaking, listening, and behaving toward others that shows that you care about them and that you are open to their ideas. Communicating respectfully, especially if there is a disagreement, requires social awareness in that students need to take the perspective of someone else in order to show respect. It also requires self-management because students need a lot of self-control so when they say what is on their mind, it's spoken in a polite and kind way. Respectful communication is critical for developing relationship skills in that students can learn how to talk with people who have different opinions than theirs and move the conversation forward, which results in learning.

WHAT DOES THE RESEARCH SAY?

A growing body of work shows that when teachers cultivate a positive, trusting climate, students experience numerous benefits. For instance, students in such classroom environments are more likely to report being socially, cognitively, and emotionally engaged in learning (Rimm-Kaufman, Baroody, Larsen, Curby, & Abry, 2015). Maintaining a positive, trusting environment requires teaching students to speak to each other respectfully in situations where they disagree. Communication of respect has two key components: (1) attitudinal, which refers to a person's attitudes, emotions, and beliefs; and (2) interactional, which refers to the way a person communicates those attitudes, emotions, and beliefs (Mackenzie & Wallace, 2011). (In this book, Chapter 3 focuses on the interactional components whereas Chapter 4 targets the attitudinal components of communication.) These features of respect are the raw material for developing competence in cross-cultural communication.

There is a rising number of programs designed to reduce racial discrimination and enhance multiculturalism in the classroom (Barrett, 2018). Whether or not schools choose to implement these programs, we know that a few of the goals of such programs can be realized by teaching socially competent conversations. When students learn how to interact with peers in a caring and sensitive manner and develop strong prosocial skills, they are more likely to show more inclusive behavior and less discrimination in the classroom (Nishina, Lewis, Bellmore, & Witkow, 2019).

Teaching Respectful Communication

A good place to start is to help students understand that it is okay to disagree. Introduce the idea that disagreements occur often during group work and that it is okay to disagree at school. Realize that families vary in how much disagreement occurs at home and how that plays out. In some families, disagreement leads to major, problematic conflict, whereas in other families, disagreement is viewed as a healthy part of family life. Some families have very little disagreement, or it is all beneath the surface and so kids are not aware of it. Know that your students will come in with varied prior knowledge about disagreement and that your role is to help them see that disagreement can be healthy and typical at school.

Poll the Class

Start with a short activity to get your students thinking about situations that may happen when they are working with others in the classroom. Say some statements about working in groups and ask your students to give you a thumbs up if they agree with the statement, a thumbs down if they disagree, and a thumb to the side if they are not sure.

Ask the following questions. Pause occasionally and encourage the students to look around the room to see if their opinions are the same as those of the other students around them.

1. Group members always have to agree with each other.
2. If you agree with someone, you should tell him or her.
3. If you disagree with someone, you should tell him or her.
4. It is okay to disagree with someone.
5. There is a respectful way to tell someone that you disagree with them.

After asking these questions, comment on what you noticed. Some students will tilt toward thinking that students in groups always need to agree with each other. If so, share with your students the idea that you do not always have to agree with each other when you are doing group work. Help them realize that people often disagree when they are doing group work and that is normal. Point out that if people in a group care a lot about their shared work, disagreements can be very common.

Discuss Respectful Disagreement

Next, talk a bit more about disagreement. Reflect on your students' answers. Discuss whether or not you should tell someone if you disagree. Help them see that it is okay to say that you disagree with someone. This is important to make explicit to children, and it helps them learn to be assertive. Talk about whether or not there are respectful ways to tell someone that you disagree with them. Dig into this a little bit and help your students understand that there are better and worse ways of stating disagreement. In doing so, you are creating a path toward learning how to take other people's perspectives.

Lead a discussion about how students can show respect when they disagree with someone. Explain that even if we disagree, we want to communicate in ways that show respect. Ask your students to think to themselves for a moment about how they could tell another classmate that they disagree with an idea. Then have the students indicate to you when they have an idea (perhaps put their thumb on their knee or their hand on their head). Next, ask your students to turn and talk to someone next to them. They can share their ideas with this partner and ask the partner how they would feel if they expressed disagreement in this way. For instance, would your partner feel respected or not so much? Reflect a little as a group.

Display and explain the image of the person in Figure 3.1. Show the difference between the thought bubble and the speech bubble. Explain how these thought and speech bubbles work. In your head, you might disagree with someone and think, "No! You are wrong!" (Point to the thought bubble.) But, instead, you pause. You wisely use respectful communication to disagree and say, "I see why you might think that. But have you ever thought of trying it like this?" (Now point to the speech bubble.)

Explain that the picture in Figure 3.1 helps you think about respectful communication. Share this idea with your students: "There have been times that I have thought something in my head [point to the thought bubble], but I realized it wouldn't be respectful to say out loud [point to the speech bubble]. Give a few examples so they get the idea. Ask your students, "Has that ever happened to you?" You may get some very humorous responses.

Explain that when you hear something that you do not agree with, it is a good idea to think and pause, then use respectful communication to learn more about the other person's idea. Explain that it is important to hear a person's whole idea before making the decision on whether it is a good idea

FIGURE 3.1. Thought bubbles and speech bubbles can differ from one another. Respectful communication can mean thinking one thing but saying another.

or a bad idea. Then point to the speech bubble and say, "Can you say more about that idea?"

For younger grades, create cardboard versions of the thought bubbles and speech bubbles in Figure 3.1. You can tape them to a wooden ruler or something sturdy. Then, as you model an internal thought, you can hold the thought bubble above your head. As you model respectful communication, you can hold the speech bubble by your mouth. Students can also demonstrate examples while holding the two signs. The hands-on element of this lesson may deepen students' learning.

Define Respectful Communication

Next, define respectful communication for your students. Respectful communication is a way of speaking, listening, and behaving toward others that shows that you care about them and that you are open to their ideas. Explain that respectful communication is important because it allows you to express your thoughts and feelings and have good relationships with your classmates.

Introduce Sentence Stems and Start an Anchor Chart

Go ahead and introduce sentence stems as a way to communicate respectfully about ideas. Explain that you will be creating and practicing sentence stems to be used when you are collaborating. These sentence stems help filter thoughts to make sure the words we choose are respectful and convey our meaning.

Start an anchor chart for sentence stems you would like your class to

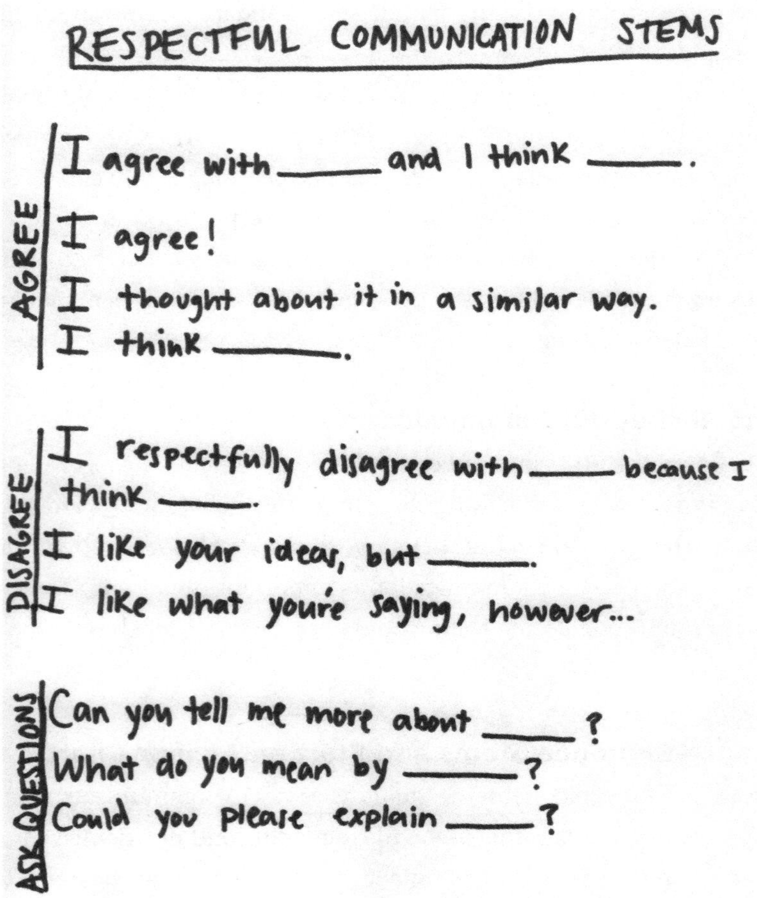

RESPECTFUL COMMUNICATION STEMS

AGREE

I agree with _____ and I think _____.
I agree!
I thought about it in a similar way.
I think _____.

DISAGREE

I respectfully disagree with _____ because I think _____.
I like your ideas, but _____.
I like what you're saying, however...

ASK QUESTIONS

Can you tell me more about _____?
What do you mean by _____?
Could you please explain _____?

FIGURE 3.2. Examples of respectful communication sentence stems.

use. Create three categories on the anchor chart (agree, disagree, and ask questions). Ask your students for input and then choose sentence stems that you think your students will be able to use well. Figure 3.2 shows an example from a classroom and can give you some ideas about what this chart will look like.

Ask Students to Generate Phrases to Use When They Agree

Start by asking students to generate and share words to use when they agree. Reword the student phrases, if needed, and write two or three sentence stems that can be used to agree, for example:

- I agree with _____ and I think that _____.
- I like what you are saying and _____.

Ask Students to Generate Phrases to Use When They Disagree

Then have students generate and share words to use when they disagree. Reword the student phrases, if needed, and write two or three sentence stems that can be used to disagree, for example:

- I hear your idea, but _____.
- I thought about it in a different way and _____.
- I'm sorry, but I disagree with _____ because I think that _____.

Remind your students that when they disagree, they need to make sure they have listened carefully so that they understand the other person's idea. Then, if there's disagreement, they can use a sentence stem like, "I hear your idea but . . . " to show respect while explaining why they have a different opinion.

Teach Students to Use Questions to Understand

Next, have students generate and share what words to use when they ask questions. Reword the student phrases, as needed, and write two or three sentence stems to use to ask questions.

Describe various ways that questions can be asked. Point out that questions help us learn more about the ideas that someone else is proposing and help us understand their line of reasoning. Instead of agreeing or disagreeing with someone's idea, asking questions helps deepen the conversation to fully understand what someone else is thinking. Mention that this is important in English language arts when they are trying to understand someone's interpretation of a book. Suggest that they can use this in science and point out that adult scientists work hard to listen carefully to other people's ideas and ask good, precise questions. Potential responses could include these:

- Can you say more about _____?
- What did you mean by _____?

Generate Examples Modeling Each Statement From the Anchor Chart

Let's say that my friend and I are talking about parks, and I think that parks with big empty spaces are nicer than parks with lots of trees. My friend might say, "I like parks with big empty spaces, because I like to play soccer and run and play." I could use a sentence stem and say, "I like what you are saying, and I think parks with big empty spaces are nice, too."

What if my friend says, "I like parks with lots of trees because I think the trees are better for the earth"? I may think that parks with trees are boring. Instead of telling my friend that she is wrong, I would say, "I hear your idea, but I like parks with big open spaces because I like to play frisbee."

Have Students Practice Sentence Stems With a Partner

Provide your students with a topic. Have each student use the sentence stem to agree with the topic. Then have each student use the sentence stem to disagree with the topic. Have each student use the sentence stem to ask questions about the topic. Choose a topic that is interesting enough to keep the students' attention but not so interesting that it will derail the lesson. Here are a few sample topics, but use what you know about your students to choose a topic that will interest them.

- I think all kids should ride the bus to school.
- I like to pack my own lunch [versus buying lunch in the cafeteria].
- All kids should have their own cell phone.

Reflect on Respectful Communication

After some student practice, call on a pair of students who have used sentence stems effectively to share with the class. Discuss how it is especially challenging to be respectful when you disagree. Ask them why it is so difficult. Talk about what students noticed about their feelings and body language when they used these sentence stems. Ask your students if they think that they will be able to use these sentence stems in other subjects when they are talking about ideas. You can point out to your students that at first, it might be a little awkward to use these sentence stems, but then it will get pretty comfortable. Also, explain that once they get the hang of this idea, they probably won't use these exact sentence stems or words but will create their own adaptations that will have a bit more natural language. Once students get used to the sentence stems, encourage these natural adaptations. I have actually heard elementary school students say, "I respectfully disagree with . . . but . . ." But students' natural language, such as, "I get what you mean . . ." might be more common.

Encourage Students to Use These Sentence Stems During the Day

Students can master the practice sentence stems but clam up when it is time to use these skills in English language arts or social studies. Remind students to apply their new sentence stem skills in upcoming days and weeks across various subjects.

STEPS FOR TEACHING
RESPECTFUL COMMUNICATION

1. Ask questions to understand what your students think about whether it is okay to disagree during group work. Affirm that it is okay to disagree because it means that everyone cares about the project.

2. Discuss how to disagree but still show respect. Show the image of the person with the thought and speech bubbles. Talk about the difference between ideas that you think versus the ideas that you say.

3. Define respectful communication.

4. Introduce sentence stems as a way to help communicate respectfully about ideas.

5. Start an anchor chart for sentence stems that you would like your class to use. Create three categories on the anchor chart (agree, disagree, and ask questions).

6. Ask students to generate words to use when they agree.

7. Ask students to generate words to use when they disagree.

8. Have students generate language to use when they want to ask questions to learn more.

9. Create a simple example. Model the use of each statement from the anchor chart.

10. Have students practice sentence stems with a partner.

11. After the student practice, call on a pair of students who used sentence stems effectively to share with the class how it worked.

12. Reflect on respectful communication. Discuss how it is especially challenging to be respectful when you disagree.

13. Encourage students to use these sentence stems in other subjects during the day.

Summary: Why Teach Respectful Communication?

Language for agreeing, disagreeing, and asking questions can have broad applications in your classrooms. Since the implementation of Common Core standards, we have seen a shift in language arts and math curricula toward more student-centered instruction. The Next Generation Science Standards and College, Career, and Civic Life (C3) Framework for Social Studies emphasize discussion about challenging ideas, discourse among students, and asking questions to unpack phenomena and the meaning of events. These new standards require students to agree, disagree, and ask questions respectfully (see the next box for some examples applied to science instruction).

It takes a lot of practice to speak respectfully to people, especially when we disagree. The example at the beginning of this chapter showed how a student included respectful language in his repertoire very naturally. Elementary school is a great time to start developing these skills. These sentence stems naturally add to students' active listening skills and can help them meet conversational challenges in the classroom and beyond. In our society, some of the best solutions arise when people with different knowledge and perspectives listen to each other, communicate respectfully, and collaborate to solve problems. Using respectful language to agree, disagree, and ask questions about other students' ideas is a key starting point toward that goal.

HOW TO APPLY SENTENCE STEMS
TO SCIENCE INSTRUCTION

Practice the sentence stems before science class and show how these stems can be used to help students engage in arguments from evidence.

Example 1: If one student is saying that plants growing in soil with compost added will grow faster than plants growing in soil without compost, another student can use the sentence stem and say, "I agree with you because compost gives the plants extra nutrients they need to grow." Alternatively, a student can say, "I thought about it in a different way, and I think plain soil has enough nutrients for the plants, so they will both grow at the same rate." Students can practice asking questions such as, "Can you say more about why you think compost helps plants grow?" Or "What did you mean when you said that compost has nutrients?"

Example 2: If one student says that paper bags are better than plastic bags, another student can use the sentence stem and say, "I agree with you because paper bags are made from renewable resources." Alternatively, a student can say, "I thought about it in a different way and I think plastic bags are better because we do not have to cut down trees to make them." Students can practice asking questions such as, "Can you say more about why people should choose plastic bags?" Or "What did you mean when you said that paper bags are made from renewable resources?"

Respecting Multiple Perspectives

The students were gathering to have a snack outdoors and just naturally sorted themselves into their usual groups and cliques. It was an ethnically diverse classroom. The white kids sat together; the three Black girls sat together, as did the two Black boys. Two Mexican students who had come to the school recently grouped up, too. Listening in, you noticed that some students were talking about their pets, others about video games, and still others about sports. This is a typical day in your third-grade classroom. The kids were behaving well, following directions, and seemed pretty happy and engaged.

These social groupings are typical and normal and even reflect healthy social interactions in the classroom. The kids are content, and you're getting a bit of a break, too. But something more is happening in these little social matchups that we need to think about. These casual moments in the classroom reflect students' natural tendency to be with people who are similar to them. This comes naturally to kids. These experiences of students connecting with people who are similar to them are important in helping them develop social skills, affirm their identity, and receive emotional support. But these naturally occurring experiences only go so far in teaching students the skills that they need to function in a diverse community, society, and world.

As a teacher, one of your roles is to support students' development by stretching them. This means helping students develop relationships with people who are different from themselves.

Teaching students to respect people with different opinions, attitudes, and ideas is a crucial first step toward functioning effectively in our increasingly diverse country and culturally complex world. Respecting multiple perspectives is not a skill we're born with—it is a skill that students can learn. With practice, students can apply this skill to their academic work and social lives. Students might be talking about a book that they are reading and can respect different perspectives on their interpretation of the study. Students might be paired up in math, have different solution paths to a problem, and see both as legitimate ways of solving the problem. On the playground and in peer interactions, students are constantly confronted with different ways of talking and being that reflect their family experiences, ethnicity or race, home culture, and family beliefs. Imagine engendering a set of skills in your students that helps them see people who are different from them as interesting and novel instead of bad or stupid. This is a lofty but obtainable goal.

What Does It Mean to Respect Multiple Perspectives?

At its core, respecting multiple perspectives means that students can identify and analyze different points of view as well as respect and value perspectives that are different from their own. By respecting multiple perspectives, students show the social and emotional skill of social awareness, meaning that they can understand the point of view and empathize with people with different backgrounds. Not only are they able to engage in this skill, but they also realize that it's important to value perspectives that differ from theirs. They recognize that not everyone has had the same experiences and as a result, their beliefs may be different, too. Because we live in a society with social stratification, social awareness can also include an understanding of inequities in society and a recognition of others' privilege or lack thereof. Students need a sense of self-awareness, as well, in that respecting different points of view requires recognition of one's own view, experiences, beliefs and privileges (or lack thereof). Students' ability to respect multiple perspectives also contributes to students' relationship skills, that is, the ability to create and maintain positive, cooperative relationships with people who are similar to and different from themselves. As students develop, these relationship skills are crucial to allowing them to negotiate conflict and resist peer pressure (CASEL, 2017). Teaching students to respect perspectives different from their own is an early stepping stone toward appreciation of diversity and tolerance of others.

The idea of respecting multiple perspectives plays out in a variety of ways in your own adult life. Think about the friends that you choose, the news that you listen to, and the activities that you choose as hobbies. Most people are drawn toward people, news, and activities that fit well with their existing opinions and beliefs. This comes naturally. There are even names for this in psychology: homophily and propinquity. We tend to develop friendships with people who are similar to us, and that's called homophily. We also tend to connect with people who spend time near us, and that's propinquity. Think about the comfort of easy friendships, our tendency to affiliate with people in our neighborhoods, and our natural gravitation toward people we know because it's comfortable. That's our comfort zone, and there's a science behind it. We naturally gravitate toward situations that are socially comfortable for us. It's easy. It's efficient. It's comfortable.

In contrast, think about times when you have stretched to get to know someone who is different than you. Maybe it was someone who was from a different generation than you are. Perhaps you pushed yourself to listen to news from a point of view that contrasts with your own. Perhaps you got to know someone of a different racial, ethnic, or religious identity. Regardless of the difference, you may have done some bridging to find commonalities in your experiences. (I am Jewish, and in an early conversation with my friend who is a Muslim refugee from Iraq, we quickly established that neither one of us eats pork.) Think back to these kinds of experiences. Were there surprises? Were you uncomfortable? What did you learn?

Let's think about how this plays out at your school when you work with different people. If you are collaborating with teachers who have different expertise and backgrounds than you do, some excellent problem solving can occur. You may teach differently and better because of a partner's insights. You may have ah-hah moments that teach you something, change your behavior, and then make you better able to reach a few students in your classroom or their family members. It makes you into a better teacher if you "share the wheel" and learn from other teachers with different expertise. In fact, it helps you grow and develop as a person to listen to others that are different from you.

Teaching students to respect multiple perspectives requires some work, but the payoff is worth it. Focusing attention on these skills helps students reinterpret some of the frustrating experiences they have when people do not see the world in the same way they do. Students are much better able to work with other students who are not necessarily their friends if they have developed skills to respect multiple perspectives. These skills can help kids approach new people and unfamiliar attitudes with curiosity and wonder.

WHAT DOES THE RESEARCH SAY?

High-quality communication among people who are different from one another requires a shift in attitudes and beliefs about people who are unfamiliar. Some classroom environments can help students understand other people's perspectives, whether others differ from them in terms of race, ethnicity, socioeconomic status, or disability status. Intergroup contact theory (Allport, 1954) forms the basis for much of the research on reducing prejudicial attitudes. The basic premise of intergroup contact theory is that four conditions need to be present for experiences to produce better relationships with people from different groups. Students need to have contact with peers who are different from them in situations where the students pursue a common goal, have equal status, notice their common interests, and are in environments that encourage intergroup contact (Allport, 1954). Translated to classroom life, this requires activities where students from diverse backgrounds work together on a common product, where each student brings valuable skills to the task so they have equal status, and where there is enough time for students to work together so they notice the emergence of common interests. These activities need to be conducted in an environment by a teacher who believes in the importance of intergroup contact for reducing prejudice. Since the development of this theory, hundreds of studies have tested ways of encouraging respect toward people who are different than them (Pettigrew & Tropp, 2006). The work has pointed to a few main findings that can be useful to teachers.

It is crucial for teachers to value diversity in their classroom for intergroup contact to reduce prejudice. In one study, the researchers examined whether students with more intergroup friendships were less likely to exclude students with special needs, and they considered teachers' attitudes in predicting this association. The findings show that the relation between intergroup friends and less social exclusion was present only if teachers saw the value in having diverse classrooms, for instance, if teachers thought the class benefited because of the diversity of students and did not believe that hetero-geneity hindered their daily routine (Grütter & Meyer, 2014). Often, teachers with all white students ask how they can reduce prejudice in their classrooms knowing that students will not experience inter-racial contact. A review of 32 research studies examined the efficacy of interventions for reducing ethnic prejudice and discrimination and revealed the value of videos and books with stories about intergroup contact for reducing prejudice (Aboud et al., 2012).

Students show benefits from both intergroup contact and within-group contact. Although many studies show the benefits of intergroup contact (Kawabata & Crick, 2011), there is also evidence for the importance of a sense of within-group belonging for sup-porting student success (Benner & Crosnoe, 2011). Further, some of these findings are quite nuanced depending on student race and the composition of the classroom (Hamm, Bradford Brown, & Heck, 2005; Wilson & Rodkin, 2011). For example, among students of color, some work suggests the importance of developing a positive orien-tation and attitude toward in-group members as critical for navigat-ing intergroup friendships (Aboud, 2003; Patterson & Bigler, 2006). The take-home message here is to embrace the reality of homophily and see the value of in-group friendship. Also, encourage students to work and play with people who are different from themselves.

Teaching Students How to Respect Multiple Perspectives

Learning to appreciate people whose worldviews are different than yours can be challenging. It is good to start with books and resources that gently guide students to understand what leads to diverse perspectives, attitudes, and opinions.

Read and Discuss a Book

Try starting with *The Sandwich Swap*. Even though this book is designed for early elementary school readers, the story will still be interesting to students in upper elementary school grades as well. Queen Rania Al Abdullah (2010) of Jordan authored the book as part of her efforts to promote cross-cultural tolerance and harmony. This book is about two girls who are best friends. They eat lunch together and like doing the same things. However, they discover differences in their sandwich preferences that create a wedge in their friendship and then become a major disagreement. The conflict escalates, which comes with arguing, drama, a food fight, and so on, and then de-escalates, which plays out through a trip to the principal's office, conversation, reconciliation, and then trying and liking each other's sandwiches.

As you read this book to your class, ask students questions about the feelings of each girl in the story. For instance, ask how each girl might have felt when her friend described her sandwich as yucky. Point to the expressions of the girls to initiate a conversation about their feeling states. Ask students if they've been in a situation where two friends had different opinions, and they felt they had to choose sides. Check in to see if they think everyone is going to like every food that they try. Get a sense from your students about whether they think it's okay to like different foods or if everyone should like the same thing. Use the book to remind students that everyone brings their own life experiences to everything that they do and that some things might be important to some people but not to others.

Here are a few useful books to teach respect for multiple perspectives in the elementary school grades. Note that the grade levels are estimates. Many of the books graded for lower elementary classrooms can be used in upper elementary grades. It can be a refreshing break to share easier texts with students, and it makes SEL more accessible to all the students in your classrooms.

- *Because of Winn-Dixie*, by Kate DiCamillo (2009), is a book about a 10-year-old, Opal, who comes home with a dog in an effort to save him from the pound. As a result of her friendship with the dog, she gets to know people and their varied points of view in her new neighborhood in Florida. The dog also gives Opal courage to talk honestly with her dad about how her mother left them. Grade level: 4–7.
- *Little Brothers & Little Sisters*, by Monica Arnaldo (2018), offers insight into what it is like to be a little brother or sister, longing to

be included by older brothers and sisters. The book profiles four sibling pairs and sheds light on how older versus younger siblings see one another. It highlights multiracial characters in an urban environment and closes with gestures of kindness from older to younger siblings. Grade level: K–3.

- *City Green*, by DyAnne DiSalvo-Ryan (1994), is about a young Black girl who starts a city garden in an empty lot. Her efforts bring out the softness and generosity of some of the more difficult members of the neighborhood. The community comes together to beautify the lot, and, as they do so, we see people's best qualities. This book about a multiracial, multiage neighborhood also includes a child in a wheelchair. Grade level: K–3.

- *Same Sun Here*, by Silas House and Neela Vaswani (2013), is a chapter book based on a delightfully honest relationship between two 13-year-old pen pals. Meena is an immigrant from India who lives in New York City, whereas River lives in Kentucky and is the son of a coal miner. Both face real life challenges—Meena's family is evicted from their apartment, and River is injured in a landslide. Their letters expose commonalities and differences and shed insight into cultural differences. Grade level: 4–7.

- *Seedfolks*, by Paul Fleischman (2009), is set in inner-city Cleveland. A young immigrant girl, Kim, plants a lima bean as a way of connecting with her late father. This leads to the creation of a garden by 13 people in this multicultural, multiage neighborhood. The empty lot transforms into a lush garden featuring vegetables from people's home countries that they cannot find in supermarkets. The garden brings members of the community together. Grade level: 3–5.

- *The Witch of Blackbird Pond*, by Elizabeth George Speare (1958), is a novel about a 16-year-old girl who leaves Barbados to live with her uncle and aunt in Connecticut in 1687. Kit does not fit easily into Puritan society; she befriends Hannah Tupper, a Quaker whom many consider to be a witch. Later in the book, Kit is accused of being a witch because of her ability to swim. The book exposes important issues about how easy it is to misinterpret the behavior of people from different cultures and backgrounds. Grade level: 5–7.

Help Students Link the Book to Their Own Experiences

Ask students to connect the experiences of the girls in this book to their own past experiences in or outside of the classroom. Ask your students about a time when they felt frustrated and annoyed by someone who liked something different from them. Perhaps they remember an argument about pizza toppings with their brother. Maybe they still cannot understand why their grandpa eats mustard. Have them reflect on those points of disagreement.

Talk about how it feels to disagree. Revisit the main point about disagreement from Chapter 3 by asking students the question, "Is it okay for people to have different points of view?" Guide them toward seeing that it is okay for people to disagree and have different points of view. Point out that our community and world would be very uninteresting if everyone liked all the same things and did the same things. You might even pull the thread on this idea and imagine: "Would we want everyone to be Cubs fans? Would it still be just as fun to cheer on your favorite team?" or "What if everybody liked the same kind of sandwich and that's all we ate every single day?"

Define Perspective and Respect

It is a good time to give students some basic definitions. Define "perspective" and "respect" because these are important terms that can come in handy. An elementary school definition of perspective means a person's point of view or how one person thinks about a situation. You might ask your students to generate a situation that they see just from their own perspective. Then, you can explain that if we only see a situation from our own point of view, then we can't learn from other people and/or appreciate other people's opinions or interests. Likewise, define respect, which means to think and act in a way that shows others you care about their feelings and their well-being. Point out that respect means that it is important to demonstrate caring about a person, even if you do not agree with their point of view. You may want to put these words on a word wall or even create a picture that depicts these ideas for younger children so you can refer to it in the future. In this conversation about words and definitions, keep the big-picture goal in mind—it's important to help students understand that differences among people and perspectives are common and make our community more interesting.

Engage in Perspective-Taking Exercises

Next, I recommend some exercises that can help students think through concrete situations in their lives where students have multiple perspectives.

The chart in Figure 4.1 shows a visual display to explore such situations with students. There are a few important elements in this chart. Each row has a sample situation with two different perspectives. Then, the figure has places to write questions that would help someone learn more about those perspectives and what people can say or do to show respect.

Create rows to generate examples that show two different perspectives on the same situation. Simply setting up these perspectives side by side demonstrates how common it is for people to have different perspectives. Make a space for students to generate questions that they could use to develop a deeper understanding of perspectives that are different from their own. Last, create a space that allows students to think about what they can say or do to show respect in light of each of these perspectives.

Walk through this example with your students so they understand the idea of two different perspectives on an issue. In talking this through, remind the students that people form their beliefs and opinions based on their own life experiences. Help them realize that not everyone has had the same experiences that they've had. For young children, this is a cognitively demanding task, which they may understand only by about second or third grade. Remind your students that we can learn from each other by asking questions about preferences. Tell them that they don't always have to agree with their friends about their ideas but that they do need to respect their friends' ideas. Show how to learn more about each other's perspectives by

SAMPLE SITUATION		WHAT ARE QUESTIONS YOU CAN ASK TO UNDERSTAND MORE?	WHAT DO YOU SAY AND DO TO SHOW RESPECT?
Perspective 1	Perspective 2		
Salma likes eating hummus and pita sandwiches.	Lily thinks that hummus and pita looks like a gross sandwich.	Does anyone else in your family like hummus? What is hummus made out of? Have you always liked hummus and pita sandwiches?	"Just like your mom eats hummus, I like peanut butter because my dad always eats it." "That's new to me. I've never heard of chickpeas before." "I can picture you as a little kid eating hummus."
Teacher-generated example 1	Teacher-generated example 1	....	....
Teacher or student generated example 2	Teacher or student generated example 2	....	....

FIGURE 4.1. Sample chart for discussing multiple perspective using *The Sandwich Swap* as a first example.

asking questions: "Why do you think that?" "What made you decide that?" Give example sentences and behaviors that your students can use to show respect to their friends: "That's interesting." "That is a new idea to me."

After the first sample situation, generate a few additional examples. Think carefully about the examples you use. Students are just learning about different perspectives, so it's important to choose examples that are not emotionally loaded. The last thing you would want is a big explosive discussion before the students have had a chance to develop skills and understand multiple perspectives. No religion, politics, banned symbols, or gendered bathroom questions until students are much more skilled at taking other people's perspectives. So, stick with the easy examples that students generate. Perhaps one student likes to eat Takis (spicy chips) and another thinks they taste terrible. Maybe one student wants to grow up and be an airplane pilot but other students think that would be a scary job. Some students like sharing a room with their brother or sister but others do not. M&Ms—do you prefer megas or minis? These are examples that will engage students but hopefully won't upset them. The goal here is to practice the skill of identifying contrasting perspectives on an issue, generating questions that can be asked to understand that perspective, and thinking through ways of showing respect to someone who holds a different perspective than your own.

Learn How to Ask Questions

Asking questions to know more about someone else's perspective is an essential skill to teach. Students will find it difficult to do this without judging and talking about their own beliefs. For example, let's consider two different points of view on eating meat. One student said she is a vegetarian, and another student said she likes to hunt. The teacher first asked students to generate questions that they could use to learn more about the vegetarian. These included: "What is your favorite vegetable? Why do you like veggies? Why are you a vegetarian?" Then, the teacher asked the students to think about questions to learn more about the person who liked to hunt. The students came up with: "Who do you hunt with? Why do you hunt? What do you use to hunt?" The teacher wrote down these questions as the kind of questions that each party could ask to learn more.

Students will need to practice asking questions to know more about other students' perspectives. You may choose to have students practice in a full group. Alternatively, you may want to have your students gather in groups of two for this exercise. Then, once the pairs are done, those pairs can join into groups of four for reflection and discussion.

Throughout this assignment, keep in mind the goals of teaching social awareness and relationships skills. Make it clear to students that it's okay to have different perspectives. People do not need to agree on everything. These different perspectives make our classroom and world much more interesting. After students complete this exercise, it would be good to help them reflect. Ask them questions to help think about perspective taking in a way that exercises their metacognition (thinking about thinking).

- Let's go back to *The Sandwich Swap.* If Lily had grown up with foods like those in Salma's house, how might things have been different? If Salma had grown up with foods like those in Lily's house, how might things have been different?

- Is it always easy to see both perspectives in every situation? What makes this easier? What makes this harder? Keep in mind that younger children will have to stretch to understand this idea, and not all of them will be able to grasp it. The goal is that students will talk about how difficult it is to see both perspectives when they feel an emotional attachment to an issue. If this question does not land well with your students, try the next question.
- Sometimes we get attached to our own perspective—so attached that we think there might be only one right way to do something. Have you had this experience? If so, were you still able to be curious and ask questions about the other person's perspective? Why or why not? Were you able to show respect toward the other person? Why or why not?

Give Students an Opportunity to Practice

Help your students learn how to take a complex and emotion-generating situation and break it down into parts. What is one perspective? What is the other perspective? How do we learn more about each point of view? How do we show respect? Having the skill to break down conflict in this way and ask these questions helps students develop a critical skill needed to get along with people who are different from themselves. You may want to do this as a large group, in small groups, or with partners depending on the age of your students and their ability to work through a table like Figure 4.1 independently.

As an experienced teacher, you may see interesting new ways to tailor this assignment to address stable conflicts and cliquey behavior in your classroom. Start with simple ideas so students learn these skills in situations that do not raise much emotion. Later, up the ante and discuss issues that are much more sensitive and emerge from cultural differences at home or differences in strongly held beliefs and attitudes. Some classrooms have students with different religions that can be explored in this way. Other classrooms have families with different beliefs that can be unpacked and discussed delicately and diplomatically. (If you choose one of these topics, be sure that you are not singling out just one or two children with that religion or beliefs; that can lead to discomfort and bullying.) Demonstrate how people can have different beliefs or perspectives but still show respect.

Ask Students to Write About Taking Different Perspectives

By fourth and fifth grade, students can write about these ideas. You may want to give them question prompts that help them think deeply. Here's a series of questions to ask:

- Write one or two sentences about a time when you disagreed or got into an argument with a friend or sibling.
- Take your friend's or sibling's perspective. What do you think your friend or sibling was thinking or feeling in this situation?
- What could you have done or said differently to respect your friend or sibling's perspective?
- If you had been more respectful, do you think things would have turned out differently?

Figure 4.2 shows an example of fifth grader's reflection on her anger toward her sister.

Student Reflection

Write one to two sentences about a time when you disagreed or got into an argument with a friend or sibling.

Once I got mad at my sister because she was breaking some pool rules. I reacted in a violent way so I had to sit out.

Take your friend or sibling's perspective. What do you think your friend or sibling was thinking and feeling in this situation?

I think my sister was feeling bad that I had to go out instead of her. But she also felt good that I was sitting out, She was laughing at me!

What could you have done or said differently to respect your friend or sibling's perspective?

I should of talked to her in a calm way. I would say, "Caroline you shouldn't do that it's against the rules."

If you had been more respectful, do you think things would have turned out differently? Explain.

Yes, we would have still been the pool with her and we both would be happy.

FIGURE 4.2. One fifth grader comes up with a solution to her sister breaking pool rules.

Integrate Multiple Perspectives Into Academics

It is also possible to integrate teaching multiple perspectives into the academic life of your classroom. Books like *Because of Winn-Dixie* and *The Witch of Blackbird Pond* introduce different perspectives. Work with your students to delve into these different perspectives and understand what they mean. For example, in *Because of Winn-Dixie*, Opal (the dog lover) has a different perspective than the landlord who orders Winn-Dixie to be sent to the dog pound. You can use the books to show the limitations of respecting multiple perspectives. Some perspectives are dangerous to have, and in those cases, you should not show respect for them. (In *The Witch of Blackbird Pond*, some people hold the perspective that Kit is a witch and should be put to death. That is an example of a perspective that can be understood but should not be tolerated or respected.) There are many examples to draw from here.

Teaching about multiple perspectives can include instruction on race and ethnicity, and these topics are not just germane to ELA and social studies instruction. A recent survey of teachers in the Richmond, Virginia area asked teachers whether multicultural topics were relevant to the subject area they taught. Among the 800+ elementary school teachers surveyed, math teachers were the least likely to view cultural diversity as an important consideration in pedagogy and curriculum (Thomas et al., 2020). This is unfortunate because existing research on pedagogy shows that teachers tend to hold lower expectations for Latinx and African American students than white or Asian American students (Tenenbaum & Ruck, 2007) and these lowered expectations have negative consequences for student self-concept and math achievement (Szumski & Karwowski, 2019). Further, recent work on equity within the mathematics curriculum has introduced exciting ways that identity and agency can be leveraged so that students of color become aware of their mathematical identity, other mathematicians in their community who are like them, and the ways in which math is rooted in ancient histories of people of color. The Seattle Public Schools are experimenting with a district-wide K–12 Math Ethnic Studies Framework (Seale, 2019) and I expect they will learn important lessons to guide future practice.

STEPS FOR TEACHING RESPECT FOR MULTIPLE PERSPECTIVES

1. Read and discuss a book that provides a good example of multiple perspectives.
2. Have your students link the book to their own experiences.
3. Define the words "perspective" and "respect" for your students.
4. Engage in perspective-taking exercises. Use a chart that gives examples of situations or beliefs that have two contrasting perspectives. For each set of contrasting perspectives, ask students, "What are questions that you can ask to learn more?" and "What do you say and do to show respect?"
5. Help your students learn how to ask questions to understand someone else's perspective.

6. Give students an opportunity to practice breaking down complex differences into simpler parts using a chart like the one in Figure 4.1.
7. With older students, ask them to write about taking different perspectives.
8. Integrate taking multiple perspectives into the academic life of your classroom.

Summary: Why Teach Multiple Perspectives?

Let us return to our natural tendency to aggregate with people who are similar to us. Think about snack time on the playground and how kids grouped together with students who were like them. That gives them practice of their regular social skills. It is useful, healthy, and typical, but as a teacher, you have the power to push for more. You can very intentionally stretch students to work, play, and communicate with students who are different than themselves. You can arrange work groups and seating situations in ways that cultivate bridges across differences. You can hold conversations that draw out the unique strengths and backgrounds of various students— these conversations may occur during instructional time or may simply add nutritive value to empty space during the day (while waiting for lunch to start). Realize your power as a teacher to facilitate students' ability to respect multiple perspectives. Just imagine if you are able to help students use their social skills to work and play with students who are very different from themselves. What could this mean for their future? Boosting students' ability to appreciate different points of view can help them become less self-absorbed, more aware of others, and more willing to question their own assumptions about what they believe. These skills provide the raw material for diplomacy and more.

Managing Frustration
and Anger

I sat with fourth grade teachers who were discussing students in their classroom. One teacher observed something surprising. She reflected on Gabriela, a very quiet student in her classroom who was new to the U.S. Gabriela was a dual-language speaker who spoke English very tentatively in the classroom. The teacher talked about how Gabriela seemed very pleasant and agreeable and got along easily with almost everyone in the class. The girl never seemed to get her feathers ruffled. Nothing seemed to bother her—not chips spilled onto her notebook by a boy nearby or the other kids all talking at once so there was no chance for her to speak up. Gabriela seemed quiet, calm, and patient.

Then, one day, the teacher did a short activity with her class to help students reflect on their strong feelings of frustration and anger. She asked students to think about different situations that could occur in their lives and indicate how strong their negative emotions would be in those situations. Examples included "Someone takes your seat at lunch," and "You lose your basketball game."

Through this activity, the teacher discovered that Gabriela was worked up about a lot of different things but just never showed it. Then this teacher looked at the responses of a different girl in her class, Isabel, who often seemed frustrated and irritated. But Isabel's written responses to this exercise reported very little frustration in the various situations presented to her.

The teacher talked about the contrast between the two girls. Gabriela was experiencing a lot of frustration and anger at school but was holding it all in. This girl was keenly aware of her internal emotional states and had excellent emotion regulation skills. In contrast, Isabel, who often moped around the classroom and showed her irritation to anyone who would listen (and some who would not), reported feeling unperturbed in the kinds of situations that might provoke a strong response. She was either unaware of her internal emotional states, had difficulty regulating her negative emotions, or both.

Instantly, the teacher began to realize some of the strengths and needs for development in these two students. Holding in emotions like Gabriela or getting easily upset on a regular basis like Isabel can reduce students' ability to concentrate and learn. Both students were experiencing or expressing emotional states that were interfering with their own learning and possibly the learning of other students in the classroom.

Management of strong emotions, especially anger and frustration, involves a variety of skills. It requires self-awareness; students need to notice the feeling from within that emerges when they start having strong emotions, and they need to understand what gets them frustrated or upset. It also requires self-management; students need to figure out ways to calm themselves down when they are feeling upset. The skill of managing emotions also involves social awareness. During the elementary school years, students become increasingly aware that their emotional expressions affect the people around them. They begin to realize that getting frustrated and angry with someone can upset that other person and may not be the best approach for dealing with a problem.

What Is Emotion Management?

As we all know, emotion management is a big deal in elementary school classrooms. One of our important roles as teachers is to help students understand and regulate (manage) their strong emotions. It is important to know a little about emotions to understand how we fulfill this responsibility. In this chapter, we focus on anger and frustration.

To start, experiencing an emotion does not necessarily mean that you actually express that emotion. Think about a time when you were so frustrated and angry about a hard situation that you felt like punching a wall. But, of course, you had students in front of you in your classroom. Instead, maybe you took a deep breath and tried to think about something else. Later, maybe you griped to a friend, stomped around, or went for a vigorous walk. This is a situation where you experienced a strong emotion (anger), but you regulated your emotion instead of expressing it badly. In this situation, you managed to hold off and express that anger in a more societally acceptable manner later that day.

Each of your students has a rich, emotional life with a full range of emotions. If you create a caring and warm classroom community, students are likely to experience happiness and joy in your classroom. Still, there will be times when they will get sad, anxious, frustrated, or angry. When they feel frustration or anger, you play a critically important role in helping them manage those strong feelings (by pausing or taking a deep breath) and expressing those feelings in a socially acceptable way (by running around the edge of the playground or using acceptable words to solve the problem).

WHAT DOES THE RESEARCH SAY?

New research considers the role of time outside and access to the natural world in children's lives. Of course, in urban settings, it can be very difficult to find any green space at all. Still, it seems important to discuss outdoor time and what it means for students. A review of research shows the benefits of exposure to natural settings at school on children's positive mood and concentration, and at home on children's attention and working memory (Norwood et al., 2019). One important study looked at green space in urban neighborhoods among children who were 3, 5, and 7. Among children from families living in poverty, those children with more access to parks, gardens, and playgrounds had fewer emotional problems, conduct problems, and peer confrontations than children with less access (Flouri, Midouhas & Joshi, 2014).

Beyond benefits to emotion management, lessons in nature appear to have other positive benefits. One team of researchers studied the effects of outdoor versus indoor science lessons on third grade learning. Teachers delivered two science lessons per week (one inside, one outside) for 10 weeks and the researchers gathered data on students' engagement in learning immediately after the lessons. After the outdoor lessons, students were observed and rated as more engaged in the next lesson and the teacher needed to redirect students' attention less frequently (Kuo, Browning, & Penner, 2018).

If you are a skeptical reader, you may wonder if experiencing time in natural settings actually causes positive behaviors or whether these two variables are just correlated to one another. As it turns out, there are some high-quality experimental studies from many places in the world to guide us. These studies show that time in natural settings can lead to improvement in attention, stress levels, self-discipline, and enjoyment in learning (Kuo, Barnes, Jordan, 2019).

After taking some time to read research on the topic, my take is that time outside can improve children's emotional state and that learning settings do not need to be that green to be considered "a green space"—a grassy patch in front of the school or an area near a few trees will be suffice. As a teacher thinking about how to help students manage their strong emotions, it can be helpful to have a lot of tools in your toolbox. Incorporating more time outside, creating time for outdoor physical activity, and trying outdoor instruction can be a few strategies to help students manage their strong emotions.

Teaching Frustration and Anger Management

Emotion management tends to develop in a particular direction during the elementary school years. In early childhood, students do a lot of co-regulating, which means students depend on the adults around them to help them manage their emotions. As children develop, they increase their ability to self-regulate, which means students become increasingly able to manage their emotions independently without support from an adult. As a teacher in your students' lives, you are supporting that development. Early on, you are an integral part of helping them calm down while also teaching them skills so they can calm themselves down. As they get older, your students have the skills needed to calm themselves down, and you can remind students to use those skills, as needed. There are individual differences, too. Some children need a lot of support (and co-regulation) whereas others have developed self-regulation skills. It is also important to keep in mind that there are cultural differences; some families value coregulation more than others and this will play out in different ways in your classroom. In addition, children who have experienced trauma often become dysregulated and need more support from adults to manage their emotions. Taken together, teachers play a very important role in students' emotion management. With this role in mind, let us turn our attention to ways that we can explicitly teach students to manage frustration and anger.

Share a Story About Feeling Frustration or Anger

Here's the kind of example you might choose:

> I was playing in a baseball game. It was the bottom of the ninth inning and my team was in the field. The game was tied and we had two outs. A player from the other team came up to bat. He hit the ball way out, but it wasn't a home run. A player starting from second base was rounding the bases and running for home. He got there in time, but he never tagged the plate—except the umpire still called him safe. I know he didn't tag the plate; everyone was complaining, but the call stood. I was furious. I was so mad. I couldn't believe it. I was so full of anger and it was so unfair. I just threw my glove on the ground and stomped off the field. It took me a long time to cool down from that. It was very hard for me to manage my emotions. Let me ask you: Have you ever felt like that before?

Next, ask your students to give you a thumbs up or thumbs down on whether they have ever felt like this before. A story like this might get your students worked up and eager to talk, so you may want to encourage them to turn and talk to a partner about a time they felt that way.

Define the Word "Emotions"

Come up with a common definition of emotions and describe how strong emotions can impact behavior. Here is a definition of emotions that works well for upper elementary school children: Emotions are feelings or mental states that come from within a person that can feel positive or negative and can have a lot of energy or only a little energy. Mention to your students that strong emotions can sometimes overwhelm us, and we may react by doing or saying things we normally would not do or say. Let your students know that they are going to learn to notice situations that bring up these strong emotions and how they can respond to these emotions.

Talk About Noticing and Managing Strong Emotions

Help your students understand that we all have strong emotions sometimes. Explain to them that they all feel frustration and anger at times and that it is normal to feel that way. Sadly, some students feel shame when they feel frustration or anger. It is important to help children realize that frustration and anger are normal and that everyone has those feelings sometimes. Explain that it is important to learn how emotions connect to our behavior because it means that some ways of showing emotions are okay, but others are not because they can hurt other people or animals or break things.

Share with students that it is important for them to learn to recognize their strong emotions. Ask your students what it feels like internally when they get angry and frustrated. Talk about these feelings—such as a tightness in their chest, mental distraction so that they cannot think of anything else, a tightening of their shoulders, fast beating in their heart, or warming in their face, ears, and neck.

Mention that they will learn some strategies for managing strong emotions that come up and can get in the way of achieving their goals. Your students may be unfamiliar with the idea of managing emotions, so you can define this term as "expressing your feelings in ways that are okay, and shifting how you are feeling so your emotions do not get in the way of your goals."

Show How a Thermometer Can Represent Frustration and Anger

Project (or draw) a picture of a thermometer. If needed, explain the general idea of a thermometer by explaining that when it is hot outside, you see the mercury in the thermometer rise. When it is cooler outside, the mercury falls. Then make the connection about how you can use the thermometer to gauge feelings of frustration and anger. Using the baseball example, you might point out that if you were to gauge your strong feelings after that baseball game, your thermometer would have the mercury at a high level.

Next, have your students take their own emotional temperatures. Ask them how they would color in the thermometer for different situations. Use examples like, "Mom cooked Brussels sprouts for dinner," "My brother does not let me play video games," or "I got home and someone ate all the jelly beans." Demonstrate how the level on the thermometer corresponds to the strength and intensity of their feelings. Once your students understand this idea, it is time for them to reflect individually on what makes them angry or frustrated.

Pass out a handout to each student with thermometers and scenarios. Figure 5.1 gives an example of what your worksheet could look like. You can

Taking Your Emotional Temperature

Read each scenario and then color in the thermometer based on how you would feel if this happened to you. A value of 10 means that you would feel really, really angry and 1 means that you would feel calm.

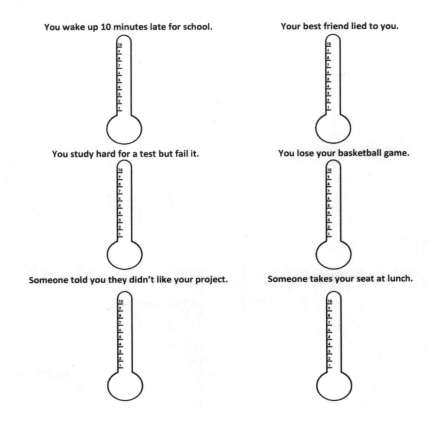

You wake up 10 minutes late for school.

Your best friend lied to you.

You study hard for a test but fail it.

You lose your basketball game.

Someone told you they didn't like your project.

Someone takes your seat at lunch.

FIGURE 5.1. This handout can help your students explore the intensity of their feelings of frustration and anger. This process of reflection helps them understand what situations lead to frustration and anger.

adjust the scenarios to match the lives and experiences of your students. Ask your students to color the thermometer to the temperature that they might feel in that situation. I recommend a red crayon or marker. When students are finished, they can share with a partner, table group, or the whole class. The students will notice that everyone has different situations that make their temperature rise. If they don't notice this, point out these individual differences to them.

Read and Discuss a Book That Models Handling Strong Emotions

The book *When Sophie Gets Angry—Really, Really Angry* (Bang, 2010) works well in discussions of strong emotions for grades K through fifth grade. In this book, a series of frustrating events happen to Sophie. Then, just when she cannot stand it anymore, her little sister takes her toy, and her mom takes her sister's side. Sophie gets very angry and runs out of the house to the ocean. As you read the book, call attention to how she deals with that anger, as well as how she manages her anger throughout the book. As you read, pause to discuss it and answer questions.

You can ask:

- How did Sophie act when she was angry?
- What did she do to make herself feel better?
- I don't have an ocean by my house; what could I do if I felt this angry?

Discuss how Sophie got angry but then was able to manage her strong emotions after doing a few things and coming back home. Point out that at the end, she felt calm and was able to come back and join in with her family as they did a puzzle. Mention how important it is to have a few techniques, like Sophie did, to help ourselves calm down so that we can get back to having fun or doing work.

Remind students that when they work in a group or have different ideas or ways of working, they can get angry or have hurt feelings. Again, help them understand that those feelings are normal and typical. You might say, "It is not bad to have negative emotions. But, with negative emotions, we need to think carefully about how we manage and express those strong feelings." Help your students understand that they need to be able to manage strong emotions so they do not get in the way of their goals and healthy relationships.

Ask Students to Generate Strategies for Managing Frustration or Anger

Ask your students to think about a time when they felt very angry or frustrated. Ask what made them feel better. You may want to have them discuss this with a partner. Then generate a list of ways of dealing with frustration and anger. Use this as a brainstorming time and write down all the positive strategies students have used in the past on a chart. Students will, of course, come up with some negative strategies that they have used, too. "Hit someone" and "Scream and yell at my sister" are popular examples. For those, help students understand why those strategies do not work and can hurt other people's feelings and get in the way of reaching their goals.

Make a Chart of Strategies That Work in Your Classroom

Either put stars on your existing list next to strategies that can be used in the classroom or create a new chart just for classroom use. (It can be nice to have this list on hand to refer students to later.) Students may describe calming themselves down with a time-out spot, squeeze balls, drawing, or other. If you are a very lucky teacher who has a door to the outside from your classroom, keep in mind how healthy it can be for kids to take a few minutes running around outside to calm down. (One of my favorite first grade teachers commonly instituted "run around," which meant running around the playground right outside her classroom three times. It worked like a charm.) We tend to underestimate the power of the outdoors and exercise to improve students' ability to manage strong emotions.

Reflect on the Chart Together

Read through the list of ideas and celebrate the great job students did thinking of ideas to calm down and feel better when they are experiencing frustration and anger. Encourage the students to turn and talk to a partner about what strategy they would like to try the next time they are frustrated or angry. Have students pick one strategy to try that week. Remind students that they can refer back to the chart if they need a reminder or want to choose a new strategy if the first one does not work.

This is a good lesson to revisit briefly from time to time. You can discuss the ideas on the anchor chart, add to them, talk about what works or does not work for different people and suggest that students try a range of strategies. You may even have your students practice a couple of the strategies when they are feeling calm. Then, when they actually are angry, they have already given the strategies deep thought and practice and will be familiar with the actions. It is important that this anchor chart does not get stale. Revisit it from time to time and keep anger management as an active part of your classroom discussion.

STEPS FOR TEACHING FRUSTRATION AND ANGER MANAGEMENT

1. Share a story about when you felt frustration or anger. Ask students if they have had similar experiences and give them a chance to discuss those experiences with partners.
2. Define and explore the word "emotions."
3. Talk about noticing and managing strong emotions.
4. Show how a thermometer can be used to represent frustration and anger. Have your students take their emotional temperature and use a handout with scenarios and thermometers to help them realize what situations make them angry.
5. Read and discuss a book that models the handling of strong emotions.
6. Ask students to generate strategies for managing frustration and anger.
7. Create a chart about the ways to manage strong emotions in your classroom.
8. Reflect on the chart together.

Summary: Why Teach Students to Manage Frustration and Anger?

Strong emotions such as frustration and anger are a part of our everyday life, especially when working and playing with others. Learning how to manage those feelings begins at birth and develops over a lifetime. Keep in mind the various components of the skills that you are trying to teach. Students need to know how to recognize and name the feelings of anger and frustration, and that process is separate from knowing how to manage those strong feelings in a socially acceptable way. You can support students' development in the full range of skills.

Keep in mind that cultures vary in how they teach children to manage frustration. Some cultures encourage children to keep these feelings inside so they do not impact others around them, whereas others encourage children to express those feelings to get them out of their system. Also, some cultures put more emphasis on co-regulation, with the expectation that an adult helps a child get back on track when they are angry, whereas others value self-regulation and expect kids to learn to manage their own strong feelings. Children bring their home experiences with them to the classroom, which can bring surprises.

A few of my students—Emily Vislosky, Frances Coolman, Mollie Lubetkin, and Rebecca McGregor—gathered completed thermometer handouts from 166 fourth graders in eight classrooms. They analyzed the students' responses by categorizing the statements into two types of situations—those that were the students' own fault versus those that were someone else's fault. On average, students had stronger negative emotional responses in situations that were someone else's fault compared to situations that were their own fault. In other words, when students felt less control over a situation and they perceived a problem as someone else's fault (e.g., someone took their seat at lunch or said they do not like their project), they got more worked up and angry than if the situation was their own fault (they studied for a test but failed it or they lost their soccer game).

This is an important idea because it suggests that it is easier to manage anger when students feel that they have some control over a situation. Notice how this plays out in your classroom. If students are frustrated and angry, it may stem from their perception of helplessness. After they calm down, you may want to reflect on that situation and help them understand why they feel helpless and, when possible, figure out a way that you can give the student more control over the situation in the future. One common issue teachers confront relates to stress from the parents' divorce. One second grade teacher described a student who was struggling through a roller coaster of emotions, including anger and frustration. Many of these feelings stemmed from confusion and helplessness, as evidenced by the student's comment that he didn't understand why his parents couldn't wait until he was grown up to get a divorce. The teacher knew that many of this child's outbursts were a result of helplessness and gave him strategies to calm down and find comfort as best he could.

The students in your classroom range in experience and expression of frustration and anger. Much like the teacher in the beginning of this chapter, you can look at your students' responses as a window into their emotional lives. Keep in mind that the quality of your relationships with your students is crucial for supporting SEL. Remember to ask your students questions about their lives. Knowing your students well can help you be attuned to what matters and motivates them. Sizing up and understanding the things that ruffle their feathers can help you prevent behavior problems that stem from frustration and anger.

Giving and Receiving Feedback

I watched two fourth grade classrooms as students gave presentations about different energy sources: coal, wind power, solar, biomass, and nuclear. As I listened, I found myself mostly paying attention to the students who were presenting. Then I looked at their captive audience. Captive, not captivated. I saw a group of bored, fidgeting yet compliant fourth graders who appeared to be sitting through the presentations waiting for their own opportunity to talk about what they learned. In the next classroom that I observed, I saw students giving similar presentations. Again, I tuned into their fourth-grade audience. Here, I saw the students engaged and interested in what the student presenters were doing and saying. I noticed members of the student audience taking notes and asking questions. Then they gave positive feedback and some constructive criticism to the student presenters. I knew that this teacher had prepared the students to use their active listening skills and to give and receive feedback in a productive way. I wanted to learn more.

As you know, student presentations are tricky. On one hand, it is great to give students the leadership and speaking experiences that come from presenting their own group project. On the other hand, what do you do about their audience? Listening to other students' presentations seems like an invitation to fidgeting, boredom, or a nap. I am glad these fourth graders did not have phones in their hands.

Keeping a student audience engaged is no small feat. I have seen teachers assign paper-based peer ratings of presentations or ask students to generate questions for the student presenters. One useful approach is to give students the tools for giving and receiving feedback. Create a culture that encourages students to be actively engage in learning and support their peers by giving positive feedback and constructive criticism.

What Is Giving and Receiving Feedback?

Giving feedback is a way of communicating with other students to help them improve their performance on an activity. Receiving feedback is a way of listening to someone who is trying to help you improve. Before students can give or receive feedback effectively, they need be in a classroom that feels safe and secure. Norms need to be in place to create that culture. Students need active listening and respectful communication skills to give feedback well.

What about receiving feedback? Again, students need to feel safe and secure. Also, students need active listening skills, and they need to exercise self-control so they do not deflect the feedback or become defensive. Once these classroom conditions and skills are in place, students are ready to exercise those skills with a new purpose—to improve the quality of their work and the work of those around them.

Learning how to give and receive feedback helps build relationship skills. Students learn how to communicate clearly, listen to another person, and cooperate to reach a goal. Students also exercise self-management as they give and receive feedback. When they give feedback, they need to control their impulses and say things in ways that will be helpful to the recipient. Social awareness is important so that students recognize the impact of their statements on other people and consider how others will interpret what they say. When students receive feedback, they need to listen carefully, manage the tendency to be defensive, and keep focused on achieving the goal they have set out to reach.

Giving positive feedback is a skill because the feedback needs to be specific and offered with the goal of helping someone else become better. Students need to listen and watch to see what their friends are doing. They need to think carefully about another student's work and attend to the details carefully. Further, they need to say things in a way that takes the other person's feelings into account.

Room for Improvement

To make feedback matter, students need to believe that the feedback they give to others can produce a better product and that work can get better over time. As we know, creating high-quality work is a process and there can be many different drafts before the final product. Kids do not learn this automatically. Most kids think that when it is done, it is done. Faster equals smarter. That's it. That is why you spend so much time teaching students about why they need to try and try again or do multiple drafts until they create a high-quality product.

To bring this idea home, think back to your own experience learning about rough drafts. For instance, do you remember learning how to write papers? It was grueling, right? In middle school or high school, did you have an ah-hah moment when you noticed your first draft was kind of crummy but your second, third, or fourth draft was actually better? Your students have not experienced that ah-hah moment yet. Until they do, you have a bit of work to do to convince them that their work can get better over time and with practice. They may need to see it in order to believe it.

Constructive Criticism

Let us shift to talking about constructive criticism. To understand why constructive criticism is so hard, we need to understand self-worth. We all care a lot about our self-worth, even if we do not want to admit it. We, as humans, run helter-skelter and go great distances to protect our sense of self-worth. We do and say amazing things to convince ourselves that we are good people even when we accidentally speed through a crosswalk while an elderly woman is waiting to cross. We go to great lengths to convince others that we are competent even if we spend five minutes looking for our phone and then realize that we are talking on it. As people, we have a natural tendency to be defensive to protect our very delicate sense of self-worth. We blame other people, make excuses, even lie—yes, we've all done it—just to feel like we are decent human beings worthy of other people's respect, love, and a good life.

This is why it is so hard to receive constructive criticism. We, as humans, like being right. Being wrong makes us feel vulnerable. We may even feel shame or embarrassment, and those are uncomfortable emotions to experience. Given these risks and our delicate sense of self-worth, let us reflect on past experiences when we received constructive criticism and it helped us grow and improve without terrible angst. What conditions were present? Who gave you that constructive criticism? How was that constructive criticism delivered? Chances are that you were in an environment where you trusted the people around you. I am guessing that the constructive criticism came from people with your best interest in mind and that the critique was delivered in a respectful and kind manner. I expect that you can create these conditions and experiences in your classroom, too. Then students will be able to give and receive constructive criticism in ways that will improve their work without creating stress and angst.

WHAT DOES THE RESEARCH SAY?

To start, let's distinguish between self-esteem and self-worth. Self-worth refers to how a person feels about their core self and their value in this world. Self-esteem refers to the sense of confidence in one's own abilities and skills. Both are vulnerable in moments when we receive constructive criticism. Here, we unpack the ideas of self-esteem and self-worth and consider how they are impacted by our own standards and the standards of people around us.

As children grow, they develop an increasingly complex sense of themselves and their self-esteem. In preschool and kindergarten, children know a few things they are good at and generally, they tend to overestimate their abilities. (They think they can jump further than they can. They think they can remember more than they can. That's just the way their minds work.) By the late elementary school years, students know that they are better at some things than others. So, for instance, they are keenly aware if they are good at math or reading and bad at basketball, for instance. As children learn more about themselves throughout development, they also adopt certain standards for their behavior and constantly compare themselves to those standards. That process of comparison between who they are and the standards that they have for themselves plays out in complex ways in school and beyond (Robins & Trzesniewski, 2005). This is the raw material for self-esteem (Harter,

2006; Harter, Stocker & Robinson, 1996; McArdle, 2009), which can in turn impact self-worth.

In early childhood, children's self-esteem reflects a set of personal standards that comes mostly from families and teachers. However, as children move through childhood and approach adolescence, their self-esteem becomes increasingly dependent on the opinions, expectations, and standards set by their peers. The same patterns of influence also emerge for self-worth. Many young people develop contingent self-worth, which means they become highly dependent on what their peers think of them in their assessment of whether they are good people or not. Not surprisingly, this can lead to dramatic mood swings. Worth noting, girls are more likely to face problems related to contingent self-worth than boys (Herrmann, Koeppen & Kessels, 2019).

Further complicating matters, children and youth start behaving in ways that match what they expect from themselves as their self-esteem becomes more task specific and consistent over time (Kernis, 2005). So, if they believe they are a weak basketball player and their peers think this to, they are more likely to avoid basketball and not try in that area. The same goes with school related topics—if peers tease and doghouse a student for being bad at math or reading, the student will underperform in that area. Here's where your guidance as a teacher is so important. Through your relationships and interactions with students, it is essential that you help individual students develop a sense of self based on their own, realistic standards, not those of their peers. Plus, set the tone in your classroom so that students feel valued and competent so that everyone has a sense of the importance of themselves and others.

Teaching Giving and Receiving Feedback

Start by sharing a time when you learned a new skill and describe how feedback was important for your improvement. Give an example, something along these lines:

When I started to dive off the diving board, I was terrified and I wasn't very good at it. My legs weren't straight, my head was too high when I hit the water, and my legs were flopping all over the place. I never seemed to hit the water at the right time. Luckily, I had a friend who was a super diver, and she helped me learn to dive better. My friend used respectful language to give me feedback and help me improve. Feedback is helpful information shared from one person to another to help them improve their performance or the product that they are working on.

Access Students' Own Experiences With Feedback

Ask students to think of a time when they received feedback that helped them improve. Your students may need a definition of feedback—something along the lines of "helpful information shared from one person to another to help them improve their performance." Discuss one or two examples as a group and explore those ideas. Ask the students what they were trying to learn, who gave them the feedback, what the feedback was about, and whether it helped them perform better in the future.

As you listen to students, carefully pay attention to what they experienced. Did they have positive or negative experiences? Did someone just heap on the praise or give them some critique to help them get better? Who gave the feedback—a stranger or someone they trust? What were the conditions of that environment? Was it a trust-filled environment where they felt good about the experience, or was it the kind of critique that they remember because it felt so awful and punitive?

Define Positive Feedback and Constructive Criticism

Then give a few definitions. Explain that there are different kinds of feedback: positive feedback and constructive criticism. Share these (or similar) definitions with your students. Positive feedback refers to compliments shared by one person with another about a performance or product. Constructive criticism refers to feedback on a person's performance or product designed to help them make their work better.

Unpack the meaning of these words so that students learn them and use them in the future. You might say that "constructive" means that you are trying to help the person be even better. "Criticism" means that you may be saying negative things about the person's work. But, put together, constructive criticism means that you are giving suggestions in a respectful way to help someone improve.

Explain to your students that if they want to give someone feedback in a way that helps them be productive in the future, they can use respectful language and give constructive criticism. Remind students of lessons learned from Chapter 3 on respectful communication.

Talk About Positive Feedback and Constructive Criticism

Discuss positive feedback and the importance of being specific in giving positive feedback. Remind students that many of them have received positive feedback and that it feels like a compliment. It can be easy to give and easy to hear.

Point out to students that they can give feedback to other students when they are giving a presentation. Give an example so they get the idea of what you mean—something like, "Oh, I like that diagram because it helps me understand a complicated idea."

Remind students that good feedback should be useful, be specific, and teach another person something important. Point out that we do not just want to say "I agree with Mary" or "Let's do that." Encourage students to be specific in their positive feedback so that the person knows what they are doing well. Ask your students to turn to each other. Have them remember a time when they gave someone useful, specific positive feedback or ask them to generate an example of positive feedback.

Next, discuss constructive criticism and explain how to communicate constructive criticism in ways that show respect. Remind them that when they give constructive criticism, they need to think about the feelings of the other person. Explain to your students that even if they don't agree with someone's idea, they need to tell them that in a respectful way. Remind them that instead of saying "I don't like that idea" or "That will never work," they can use nicer language to show respect and care.

Introduce New Sentence Stems

Share an anchor chart with sentence stems for students to use while giving positive feedback and constructive criticism to their peers. You may want to start with some of your own and then add some of their ideas to save time. Examples for positive feedback include these:

- I was interested when you said . . .
- I liked how you . . .
- My favorite part was . . .

Ask your students to generate a few additional sentence stems for positive feedback. Then, share some sentence stems for constructive criticism, such as these:

- I need to hear more about . . . because . . .

- I like . . . but I didn't understand . . .
- Next time you could try . . .

At first, use sentence stems with your class. Once they have practiced giving positive feedback and constructive criticism, they will be able to use kind, natural-sounding language instead.

Give an Example Scenario

Provide a scenario and invite students' feedback. Have some fun here. My favorite example to use is joke telling. Explain to your students that you want to be a better joke-teller. Tell your students that when you tell a joke, people look bored or uninterested, but you want them to be happy and entertained.

Then tell a joke or story in a way that is not entertaining or is missing information. For example, do not give enough time for the punchline, say the joke with a facial expression or tone that makes it not funny, or tell a joke that is boring because everyone already knows it. Ask them to use the sentence stems to give you positive feedback.

Here is my all-time, award-winning favorite for telling a joke badly:

Me: Knock knock.
Students: Who's there?
Me: Interrupting cow.
Students: Interrupting cow who? [Long pause here.]
Me: Moo.

If your students know this joke, they will love hearing it told badly. They will give you constructive criticism like, "Why don't you say 'moo' while we're saying 'interrupting cow'?" and "Maybe you should make a moo sound instead of just saying 'moo.'"

In case you are not fond of cow humor and you are a little low on not-so-funny jokes, here are a few examples:

Q: What did the left eye say to the right eye? **A:** Between us, something smells.

Q: Why did the student eat his homework? **A:** Because the teacher told him it was a piece of cake.

Q: Why does a seagull fly over the sea? **A:** Because if it flew over the bay, it would be a bay-gull.

Q: What animal is always at a baseball game? **A:** A bat.

Ask Your Students for Feedback and Model Listening

Remind your students of your goal—to become better at telling jokes. Ask them for positive feedback first. Remind them that you want encouragement because you are trying to get better at this. Ask them to be specific so that you will show improvement. Ask them to use the sentence stems.

Listen to the positive feedback. Smile, nod, and receive the feedback gracefully. Ask the students to notice how you are receiving feedback (e.g., "You see, I'm smiling." "I'm nodding." "I am saying 'thank you.'").

Ask your students for constructive criticism. Encourage them to use the sentence stems. Listen to the constructive criticism and smile or keep a neutral face. Nod and receive the constructive criticism well. Say "thank you" after hearing the criticism. Ask the students to notice how you are receiving feedback.

Point out that you are receiving the constructive criticism in a way that shows that you are grateful for the feedback. Indicate that you are smiling, nodding, and saying, "That's a helpful idea," not, "Oh, you're wrong—my joke is really good." Comment that you are not getting sad about the critique but that you are accepting the critique and considering if and how the ideas might help you improve. Mention that there are certain words that you can say when someone is giving you constructive criticism, for example, "Thank you, that will help my project," or "That's very helpful."

Tell the Joke Again and Reflect

Retell the story or joke using their comments. Ask them to offer more positive feedback and constructive criticism. Afterward, reflect with your students. You might point out that when someone asks for advice to improve, they are making themselves vulnerable. They are inviting someone to critique them, which can make them worry. But actually they are asking for your help, so it is important to be kind and offer that support. This is a great place for students to practice the skills they developed in taking multiple perspectives.

Practice Giving and Receiving Feedback

Generate a topic or activity for students to practice using sentence stems. Remember that using sentence stems for the first time takes concentration, so choose a simple topic or activity and make sure it is one in which students do not feel highly invested. For instance, have each of them describe the process of a simple task like making a bed or tying shoelaces, as opposed to solving a math problem with a single correct answer. Asking students to draw a picture with their nondominant hand is an activity that works well for this exercise. Just make sure the sentence stems you have generated work well with the activity, or students may be distracted by the awkward wording.

Let students choose a partner. Have each student use sentence stems to give positive feedback. Then have each student use stems to give constructive feedback. Ask them to practice giving feedback. Remind students to receive the positive feedback with a nod, smile, or "Thank you." Ask them to use the sentence stems to practice giving constructive criticism. Remind students to receive the constructive criticism with a nod or simple statement.

Reflect as a Class

As a group, reflect on giving positive feedback and constructive criticism. Discuss the way that feedback can help improve other people's ideas. Mention that when we work together, in any capacity, it is important for us to give feedback to each other so that we can grow.

Talk about how it felt when they gave and received positive feedback. Discuss what it was like when they gave and received constructive criticism. Give some concrete examples. So, for instance, if you want your students to give feedback when their peers are giving presentations, talk about the language they could use. If they are watching a presentation and thinking,

"Wow, maybe they should have put a picture on that poster so we know what it looks like," they can suggest, "Next time you could try using a picture on your poster to help me understand." Suggest the use of a "feedback sandwich." That is, start with positive feedback, then give constructive criticism, and then end with positive feedback.

STEPS FOR TEACHING HOW TO
GIVE AND RECEIVE FEEDBACK

1. Ask students to think about a time when they received feedback that helped them improve.
2. Explain and define positive feedback and constructive criticism.
3. Discuss positive feedback and constructive criticism.
4. Introduce sentence stems for positive feedback and constructive criticism.
5. Give students an opportunity to give you feedback and model a positive response to that feedback. Telling a joke badly works. Invite both positive feedback and constructive criticism from students.
6. Ask your students for feedback and model listening.
7. Do your activity (like telling a joke) again. Do it better this time and reflect with the class on the impact of their feedback.
8. Ask students to practice giving and receiving feedback.
9. Reflect as a class.

Summary: Why Teach Giving and Receiving Feedback?

We know that learning is a process and that our work gets better with feedback from people around us. However, for peer feedback to work in your classroom, students need to trust each other, hone their skills at giving and receiving feedback, and believe that feedback is valuable for creating a better product. Despite the fact that giving and receiving is a fairly complicated skill, once students have practiced active listening and respectful communication, they will be ready to apply those competencies to give and receive feedback.

It is especially important to encourage peer feedback. Students learn content from looking at another student's work carefully and critically, and facilitating peer feedback is a way of increasing their engagement in a variety of different learning activities. By teaching students how to give peer feedback, you are increasing the amount of time each student spends focused on content. That kind of engagement can enhance their understanding of the material.

Yet another reason for encouraging peer feedback is that it flattens some of the hierarchies that naturally exist in the classroom. As a teacher, it can be easy to forget that there are power differentials within your classroom, but they are truly present, and they impact children's ability to concentrate and learn. It is hard to learn if you feel like everyone around you is more important or deserving than you are.

Dominance hierarchies are established and sustained inside and outside the classroom. These hierarchies may reflect social stratification present in the culture. Some students may be viewed as more important than others because they have an expensive backpack, or their family has a lot of status in the community, or they are especially smart. "White privilege" is likely present in your classroom. Alternatively, hierarchies can also reflect popularity and power as it plays out in the microcosm of your classroom. At times, it may be challenging for teachers to understand the standards upon which power differentials are based.

What is important to realize is that students are extremely attuned to the haves and have-nots in the classroom. They know which kids learn things quickly. They know which kids have more power. And, of course, they know which kids get more of your attention. Hierarchies in the classroom are reinforced through simple words, glances, gestures, and other subtle signals. Even by first grade, students know who is in the high reading group or better at math (though their assessments may not be accurate). By the time students are in fifth grade, they are acutely aware of academic and social hierarchies.

As a teacher, you cannot completely stop these social hierarchies from playing out in your classroom. But you can flatten the hierarchy by pointing out each student's strengths, sharing your attention equitably among the students in your classroom, and explicitly addressing insults and putdowns that exacerbate dominance issues.

Encouraging peer feedback is yet another tool that you can use to reduce power differentials in the classroom. Every student can be prepared to give feedback to every other student. Likewise, every student can be prepared to accept feedback from any other student. If you are attuned to students' individual strengths, you can call attention to those strengths and use that information wisely as you mix and match and figure out who gives feedback to whom on what. For instance, a student with excellent visual skills may be terrific at giving feedback on another student's graphs, figures, or pictures. A student whose dad drives a bus may be primed to think through a student's draft version of a paper on city transportation. As a teacher, you act as the "invisible hand" in peer social interactions (Farmer, Lines, & Hamm, 2011) and have remarkable ability to level hierarchies.

Power differentials matter in the classroom because constructive criticism is tough to hear, and certain social conditions need to be present for constructive criticism to be productive. This criticism can be uncomfortable, and it takes time for students to learn how to accept it without feeling like it is an attack on their self-worth. Yet life is full of opportunities to give and receive feedback. Even job references often involve a question, "How does this person take feedback?" and they certainly are not talking about positive feedback. Work through this lesson and create opportunities for student practice. With time, your students will be able to give and receive positive feedback and constructive criticism in ways that show critical thinking, respect, and caring for one another.

Persevering

I was observing a sixth grade math class. At the end of the day, the teacher asked the students to complete a short survey reflecting on how much they showed perseverance during their math class in the past quarter. The teacher explained that he would be adding this to the students' folder to discuss with parents in the student-led parent-teacher conference. One student was goofing around and writing silly things on the survey. The teacher approached the student, crouched down to his level, and said, "Let's talk about how math class has been for you this quarter. Let's think carefully about the information that you might like to share about your experience in the classroom." The student got serious and then looked a little sad and disappointed. He recalled to his teacher that he didn't do well on two quizzes right in a row and that he didn't have anything good to put on the survey. Then the teacher prompted the student's memory. "Remember what happened after both of those quizzes. You asked to retake the quizzes and you did better the second time. Even when you looked frustrated because things didn't turn out just like you hoped, you calmed yourself down and then tried again. Sometimes you asked for another explanation about how to do the problems, and one time you did extra practice problems. For both quizzes, you did better the second time that you took them. I've seen you work very hard in this class. I know there are things you can be proud of!" The student nodded his head and returned to his survey. The student was not aware of his own perseverance until his teacher pointed out this accomplishment.

After watching this scene play out, I understood why the student was goofing around. He was having a hard time seeing that anything that he did in math class amounted to much. But the survey asked the students to reflect specifically on their perseverance, and this student tried and then tried again. He showed improvement as he worked. Even though the student did not see this as an important achievement, the teacher called positive attention to the student's perseverance and prepared the student for future challenging situations.

Consider for just a moment the many ways that you have persevered in your own life. Your electronic gadgets break and need to be repaired. Tax forms are hard to figure out. Returning to school to pursue a graduate degree means writing challenging papers and taking exams. New curricula take time to learn and master. Some students in your classroom need repeated reminders plus explanations over and over until they understand what you are saying. Raising kids is a continual test of patience. All these situations require perseverance on your part. As you approach these challenging situations, you may feel a strong wave of negative emotions coming on. Somehow, you manage to pause, control your strong feelings, step back, reaffirm your goal, and try new strategies to conquer problems so you can achieve your goal. All this takes perseverance.

In Chapter 5, we discussed how to help students manage strong emotions like frustration and anger. We looked at strategies to help students become aware of their feelings, the impact of those feelings on their behavior, and ways of managing those strong emotions. Teaching perseverance is the next natural step. In this chapter, we expand upon those self-management skills by supporting students to strive to work toward a goal, despite the barriers and negative feelings that may arise.

The teaching of perseverance helps student develop self-awareness in that they become able to accurately recognize their emotions and understand how those emotions relate to their behavior. Perseverance also requires self-management in that students have to learn to regulate their emotions, thoughts, and behaviors so they stay motivated to pursue long-term goals. Our goal here is to help students recognize and name the feelings that accompany difficult work. Also, we want them to apply strategies to persevere in their academic work in the classroom. School and life present all kinds of obstacles. With children, we need to help them recognize this reality and teach them how to overcome obstacles to achieve their goals.

Through the strategies in this chapter, students will learn that negative feelings such as frustration and disappointment can occur when work gets difficult. They will also learn that perseverance means continuing to work toward a goal even in the presence of those negative feelings. You can help them develop the understanding of what perseverance is all about. Then, they can begin to practice persevering and eventually notice situations that require perseverance and apply their new skills.

WHAT DOES THE RESEARCH SAY?

Many people are familiar with research on growth mindset. Unfortunately, this research is often interpreted incorrectly. Here, I give some definitions and describe the growth mindset idea with accuracy. Dweck (1999) and colleagues differentiate between fixed and growth mindset; a student who believes that intelligence cannot be changed shows a fixed mindset. When students believe that they can change their intelligence, they show a growth mindset. Students are more likely to persevere in situations where they have a growth mindset because they feel a sense of agency (that is, they feel like they can create change through their actions). Teacher praise communicates the cause of high performance to students. "You did well on this assignment because you're so smart" suggests that high performance is because of an inner, stable quality that they hold. If you say, "You did well on this assignment because you worked so hard," it communicates that their effort led to their high-quality work.

One major finding in education research is that boys outpace girls in math achievement (Robinson & Lubienski, 2011). Mindset gives us some insight into why this occurs. When students are solving challenging math problems, there is a moment when they feel confusion. In response, they interpret their feelings of confusion by either applying a fixed mindset and thinking, "This is a tough problem, and it's too hard for me," or applying a growth mindset and thinking, "This is a challenging problem, so I'll need to work harder to solve it." This momentary feeling of confusion is extremely common. Research suggests that the girls with the highest abilities are most likely to use a fixed mindset to interpret their confusion at a crucial time in problem solving, resulting in diminished sense of agency in math and more attrition from the field (Dweck, 2007).

There are misconceptions about mindset that are important to understand as you cultivate perseverance in students (Dweck, 2015). First, it is not enough to praise students for effort. We also want to teach students a variety of strategies to solve problems when their first solution does not work. When you tell students to persevere, they tend to repeat the same action to solve a problem. Just repeating the same action over and over will not work; students will not solve the problem, and then they will feel helpless. Instead of focusing just on effort, try giving students a broad range of strategies to solve problems. Ask students, "What have you done so far? What has worked or hasn't worked? What else could you try?" and encourage students to ask themselves these questions.

Second, having a growth mindset means that you need to react to mistakes and problems as opportunities for growth and learning. Often, our immediate reactions to students' mistakes is that they are problematic or harmful. It is hard to unlearn this deep-seated habit. Instead, as teachers we need to learn to respond to mistakes by pausing and pointing out the ways that the mistakes can be helpful for learning. Third, it is important to keep in mind that all adults have growth mindsets about some things and fixed mindsets about others. It is tempting to try to convince yourself that you have a growth mindset toward everything. Instead, be reflective and unpunishing about your actual feelings. Notice your fixed mindset thoughts when you have them and size up if, when, and how you could tilt toward a growth mindset.

Teaching Perseverance

Begin by reading a book with a lesson about perseverance. I recommend *The Most Magnificent Thing* by Ashley Spires (2014). In this book, a young girl aspires to make a wonderful, magnificent thing. I won't say what she's making—no spoilers here. She runs into all kinds of problems in her pursuit, and she gets upset and angry. Then her dog reminds her to go take a walk. She calms down, returns to her work, and achieves her goal. As you read, mention to your students that they may feel some connection to the main character in this book. Also, this book can be used to teach context clues or other literacy skills. It includes interesting words like tinker, pounce, wrenches, fiddles, nudges, tweaks, and pummels that you may want to explain to expand your students' vocabulary.

As you read, stop to highlight feelings the character is experiencing and ask your students if they have ever experienced similar feelings. Emotions mentioned in the book include frustration, anger, defeat, relief, aggravation, irritation, nervousness, jitters, upset, and tension. You may want to work with your students to define these emotions as you read. Talk about the way the girl in the story handled all these emotions so that she could keep working toward her goal. Help your students understand that emotions become easier to handle if you can recognize and name them. Keep in mind that we want to help students move from describing their emotions as simply bad toward more nuanced definitions such as frustrated, aggravated, anxious, or jittery. Ask your students what advice they would give to the girl at the point in the story when it seems the girl has given up on her project. This will help your students be ready for a conversation about perseverance.

Define Perseverance

Introduce the idea of perseverance to your students. Explain that perseverance means working hard and trying your best to accomplish a goal, even when the work is difficult and you face challenges. Then help students label the feelings that they have had when work becomes difficult.

First, focus on the negative feeling states that come with work. Encourage students to use a variety of different words to describe these feelings as a way of supporting their understanding of emotions that can occur when working toward a goal. Support students' emotion categorization by defining these negative feelings. Talk about how negative feelings can make people want to quit. Close the conversation by pointing out optimistically that we have the power to recognize these feelings, change our attitude, and persevere.

Refer back to your earlier lesson on managing strong emotions in Chapter 5. Sophie, in the book *When Sophie Gets Angry—Really, Really Angry*, took a walk to calm herself down. Talk about how a walk like this might help her refocus. Point to the anchor chart you created a few days or weeks ago with a list of ideas for ways to manage strong feelings like frustration and anger. Suggest some of the text-to-text connections that you can make here between *The Most Magnificent Thing* and *When Sophie Gets Angry*. You can talk about how these characters experience feelings of frustration and discuss how the books are similar or different. The take-home message here is that strong feelings can get in the way of our progress, and it is important to notice and then manage those feelings.

Talk About Perfectionism

My guess is that you have some students in your classroom who are perfectionists. This tendency can interfere with their willingness to try because they are too afraid to fail. Over time, this can mean students take less initiative, which can be problematic. This is a classic situation where children's negative feelings can interfere with their success. Since *The Most Magnificent Thing* is dedicated to perfectionists, it opens up a perfect opportunity to define and discuss the idea of perfectionism. Here is a child-friendly definition for upper elementary grades—a perfectionist is a person who holds very high standards for their own performance and may become upset by something that has a mistake or is not perfect. Ask your students if they have ever had an experience of being a perfectionist. Have them describe the feeling that goes with that perfectionism and point out the ways that perfectionism can get in the way of their own progress. If students have difficulty generating their own examples, suggest writing, since so many people struggle with perfectionism in this domain, something along the lines of, "Sometimes when I am writing I want everything to be just right. But when I am so focused on the perfect story I end up with a blank piece of paper, and I don't get any of my great ideas written at all. This can frustrate me even more. My perfectionism gets in my way when I am trying to do work."

Now that you have talked about managing the negative feelings that can come up in projects, explain the importance of perseverance and not quitting when the work gets hard. Remind students that it is important to choose goals and work toward them, even if barriers come up. Talk about different ways of accomplishing goals. Encourage students to pause, think, and note, "This strategy is not working. Is there a different strategy that I can use to achieve my goal?" This process of trying, pausing, making adjustments, and trying again is an incredibly important skill for students to learn.

Create an Anchor Chart to Guide Future Work

Together, create an anchor chart that illustrates what perseverance looks and sounds like. Start by writing down the definition of perseverance and then

In our classroom, perseverance...

Looks Like 👁	Sounds Like 😊
· Trying hard	"Keep trying"
· Working through a problem	"Think of another way to..."
· Being focused	"Good job!"
· Taking a break and coming back to it	"Don't give up."
· Trying new strategies	"Try your best."
· Doing your part and more	"Try sharing ideas with someone else..."

Perseverance is working hard and trying our best to accomplish a goal, even when the work is difficult and we face challenges.

FIGURE 7.1. Here is a sample anchor chart. While we often recommend trying and trying again, this anchor chart also suggests trying new strategies. Students need to learn that trying hard is not enough, but that you need to try different approaches to get to a solution.

generate ideas from students in your class about what perseverance looks like. "What would I see you doing when you are persevering or helping someone else persevere?" Examples I have heard before include trying new strategies, drawing or making a model, staying focused, asking new questions, seeking out resources, making a list of the things that are working and the things you need to change, and taking a short break to clear your mind and then sitting back down to work.

Then ask your students to generate ideas about what perseverance sounds like. Ask, "What are some things I would hear you saying if you were encouraging others to persevere on a difficult project? What would you say to someone who is struggling or frustrated? What could you say to yourself?" Write the students' responses on the chart (Figure 7.1). Common examples include, "You can do it. Don't give up." "I've almost got it. I know I can do this." Talk with your students about how they might feel if they heard people say this. Help students understand that hearing these kinds of statements may make them feel motivated and encouraged to accomplish a task.

Create a Persevering Classroom Culture

Here you have an opportunity to create a persevering classroom culture. You can ask your students to watch each other's behavior. This is a great opportunity to highlight some great habits among students in your class, especially for those who are usually not the center of attention. Ask students to watch their classmates and catch them persevering. Tell them to watch everyone in the class, not just their close friends. When they see signs of perseverance, they can write that student's actions on a sticky note and add it to the chart. Encourage your students to think broadly about when this could occur—it could be in math class when someone is working on a tricky multiplication problem, or it might be in gym class when someone is running the mile. By choosing a variety of settings, you will get a bigger range of actions and students. You, too, can catch students persevering, and you may want to note students who are unlikely to be recognized by their peers or may need a little positive attention to strengthen their resolve.

Persevering can be linked to the English language arts curriculum in many ways. For instance, you can link it to academic content as you teach about character traits, connections, cause and effect, and context clues. Ask students to write about a time they showed perseverance. Then ask students to consider and write about what would have happened if they had given up.

Model Perseverance

As we know, persevering is not just for students. Teachers run into so many opportunities to model perseverance to their students. When you're having difficulty with your SMART Board, talk about the process of persevering aloud. You can talk about the ways that you are managing your frustration: "Now, I'll take a deep breath." Then you can show them how you try a few different strategies to reach your goal: "Let's push this button. And this other button. Let's unplug and replug. Now I'll go ask someone for help." If you are frustrated, but calm enough to make this request, you can even ask your students to remind you to persevere and point out that we all need encouragement sometimes.

STEPS FOR TEACHING PERSEVERANCE

1. Define perseverance.
2. Talk about perfectionism.
3. Elicit responses from your students to create an anchor chart about what perseverance looks like and sounds like in your classroom. Add the definition of perseverance to the bottom of the chart.
4. Create a persevering classroom culture.
5. Model perseverance in the classroom.

Summary: Why Teach Perseverance?

Learning and working together requires caring, respect, and understanding people with different points of view. Those skills alone will not work unless students know how to persevere in challenging situations. The intensity of negative feelings can be very strong as students face barriers. To save face and protect feelings of self-worth, it is easier to give up instead of persisting. In the early grades, students learn to persevere as they learn to read, tie their shoes, and navigate disagreements with their friends. As students progress through elementary school, they will need to be able to work on longer and harder assignments with long-term goals in mind. Many of the projects that they will work on inside and outside of school will require them to work with others as they pursue goals. You will know that perseverance has taken hold when students become peer motivators and offer words of encouragement to their fellow classmates. The ability to persevere despite barriers is an essential skill.

Some students will come to your classroom with a natural tendency to persevere. They may have been born with a temperament that makes it easier for them to manage frustration. Maybe their families or previous school experiences supported their development of these skills. As you size up who has an easier versus harder time persevering, keep in mind that perseverance involves a few components, including an emotion management element and a sustained effort element. These elements create two reasons why students stumble in their efforts to persevere and work toward a goal.

Let's go back to the anecdote at the beginning of the chapter. Remember, students were asked to respond to a survey reflecting on their perseverance in math class. One student started goofing around and laughing instead of responding to the survey. This does not surprise me at all in that goofing around is a great distraction from a seemingly unpleasant task. It is also worth mentioning that students do not naturally recognize their ability to persevere, nor do they see it as a strength. Elementary school students have difficulty describing the negative emotions that come up as they persevere. They have difficulty verbalizing the exact reason they are giving up on a goal and why it is difficult to persevere in challenging situations. That is where magical teachers come in. By describing, narrating, and teaching about the process of persevering, students develop the language and skills needed to try, try, and try again.

Here are some books about perseverance. Many of them are multicultural, allowing you to match your students' ethnic background or stretch students to learn about other cultures that may be unfamiliar to them. As mentioned in Chapter 4, some of these books targeted to students in K–3 are also terrific read-aloud options for students in higher grades.

A Dance Like Starlight by Kristy Dempsey (2014) is a touching book about an African American girl living in an urban environment who dreams of becoming a ballet dancer. In this story set in the 1950s, the girl is told that Black girls cannot dance onstage. The girl's mother points out that dreaming upon a star is not enough to make wishes come true but that reaching your goals requires hard work. The girl is inspired by the African American ballerina Janet Collins, who performs at the Metropolitan Opera House, thus breaking racial barriers. Grade level: K–3.

Emmanuel's Dream, by Laurie Ann Thompson and Sean Qualls (2015), is based on a true story of a boy from Ghana, born with only one working leg. His mother, Mama Comfort, taught him that "he could have anything but he would have to get it for himself." As a boy, Emmanuel conquered great challenges despite his disability. His school was two miles from home, yet he hopped there and back on his own. He learned to play soccer, worked many jobs, and eventually became a cyclist. Now, as an adult, Emmanuel leads an organization to empower people with disabilities. Grade level: K–3.

Flight School, by Lita Judge (2014), is about a penguin that goes to flight school to learn to fly because he has "the soul of an eagle." The teachers tell him penguins aren't built to fly, but he tries anyway and fails. The teachers put feathers on him and tie him to a flamingo so he can fly. The penguin is delighted. At the end of the book, he comes back with his friend the ostrich to learn to fly. Grade level: K–3.

Richard Wright and the Library Card, by William Miller (1997), is a fictionalized story about Richard Wright, author of *Native Son* and *Black Boy*, and his perseverance. This book describes Wright living in the segregated South in the 1920s. He wants to borrow books from the library but is not allowed to because of his race. He perseveres and gets help from a coworker, eventually giving him access to books. Grade level: K–5.

Ruby's Wish, by Shirin Yim Bridges (2015), is a book about an ambitious girl from old China. At that time, most girls in China aspired to get married, but Ruby strives to attend a university and get an education like her many brothers. Ruby's family supports her goals and rewards her for her perseverance. The book is based on a true story of the author's grandmother. Grade level: K–3.

The Star People: A Lakota Story (Nelson, 2003) is about a

Lakota Indian girl who gets lost after surviving a prairie fire and following dynamic clouds created by the Cloud People. After several mishaps that create opportunities to persevere, the Cloud People receive guidance from a deceased grandmother, whom they dearly miss. She guides them back home. This book sheds light on Native American culture and also gives an example of how the felt presence of a deceased relative can lead to perseverance. Grade level: K–3.

With any of these books, you can link to language arts instruction by talking about character traits, connections, cause and effect, and context clues. These books lend themselves to an assignment involving students to write about a time they showed perseverance. Students can give the stories two alternate endings, one in which they persevered and another in which they gave up.

Resolving Conflict

An upper elementary teacher was giving a lesson on different strategies to resolve conflict. She asked students to write about a time when they experienced conflict. Wisely, she said, "If you cannot think of a conflict in your own life, you can share one that you know about." She added, "Some of you will be talking about these conflicts with the class, but if you are writing about one that you do not want to share, you can say 'pass.'" The students wrote about the conflicts they or their friends had experienced and began to share and discuss those conflicts. One boy said, "One day, someone brought up my sister in a bad way," meaning that someone said something mean about his sister. "Then I talked about them in a bad way. The teacher told us we had to go into the time-out room and talk it out. He said he was sorry. I said I was sorry. But we were both still mad. Then one day at a soccer game, I called him for my team. Then, after that, we got along better." The teacher talked about the scenario and discussed all the bad feelings that come from saying mean things about each other. Then she pointed out that it can take time to work out tough situations like this. She gave praise, attention and appreciation to the student who worked this out.

Conflict in the classroom is inevitable. Especially when students are working together on a collaborative project, there is no way to avoid disagreements, problems, and arguments. But that very inevitability presents an opportunity for students to practice so many of the social skills that we want them to develop. If you ask your students to do more group work, they are going to have social interactions across a wider variety of students in the classroom than just their friends. This may lead to more conflict. Fortunately, there are strategies that you can use to be proactive and teach students to resolve conflict with aplomb.

What Is Conflict Resolution?

Conflict resolution involves identifying the source of a conflict and taking steps to resolve it. This complex skill follows naturally from many of the simpler skills your students have learned so far. Active listening, respectful communication, respecting multiple perspectives, and managing strong emotions will all be important in learning how to resolve conflict. Students develop relationship skills as they learn to resolve conflict. They learn constructive ways to assert themselves and resolve tough situations while maintaining high-quality relationships. They practice self-awareness, self-management, social awareness, and decision making, too. As a teacher, you spend a lot of time helping students resolve their disagreements. Ideally, as your students get older and develop more skills, they will learn to resolve their conflict independently.

Take a step back and consider the wide range of competencies it takes to resolve a disagreement. Students need to notice the discord, stay calm but get energized to cope with the situation, feel deserving and important enough to assert themselves, use language skills effectively, and convey respect in what they say so that they do not make the conflict even worse. They need to manage the strong feelings that come with wanting one thing when they know another student wants something else. Students need to be able to think about different solutions for problems and consider the consequences of their choices. Further, students need to take other people's perspective and understand that other people have different preferences and see the world differently. Beyond just having skills, students need to value other people in their classroom community. Without valuing others, they will not be motivated to address conflict in a way that keeps high-quality relationships intact.

The need to resolve conflict in classrooms is obviously not a new idea. In fact, there are many programs and that provide strategies and multi-step approaches to resolving conflict. The approach that I describe here is based on the "Gordon Model" in Teacher Effectiveness Training developed in the 1960s (Gordon, 1975). What I have discovered is that many different approaches to conflict resolution share commonalities with the Gordon Model (Denton & Kriete, 2000; Therapist Aid, 2020).

Assertiveness Is Critical for Conflict Resolution

One aspect of conflict resolution especially deserves our attention—assertiveness. Think, for a moment, about times when you have not resolved a conflict. Consider the situations in which you have said, "Let sleeping dogs lie," which basically translates to noticing that something is bothering you but deciding not to do anything about it because you feel uncomfortable about asserting yourself or you're too worried about offending someone or messing up an otherwise high-quality relationship. This is, unfortunately, very common, but too few people spend time thinking about the importance of asserting oneself.

As you read this, you may be chuckling about the students in your class who definitely do not need help in learning to assert themselves. No doubt you have some students who have a lot to say. They argue their points and maybe get their way a little too often. Some of your students are so good at asserting themselves that they act like they deserve unusual levels of attention and special treatment. These students do not need help learning to assert themselves. They may instead need help understanding that their constant assertiveness is challenging to their relationships with people around them.

Let's put those students aside for a minute and think about some of the students whom you know less well. Consider the quietest students in your class. Do they have the skills needed to assert themselves in a disagreement? Reflect on whether you have students in your class whose opinions are eclipsed. Are there some students who just naturally go with the dominant opinion? Are there students who seem content to follow another student's lead? It is possible that these students are comfortable with other people making decisions for them, but it's also possible that they lack the skills to be assertive.

The problems get deeper when we consider that hierarchies and stereotypes that exist in society can play themselves out in the classroom. In many classrooms, students of color have gradually learned that white kids get their way more than they do. In some spaces, students feel unknown or unrecognized because their race is not represented in the leadership of the school, their teachers, or the books and materials in the classroom. Although teachers may not be aware of it, girls often get less attention than boys. What about students from other traditionally marginalized groups? For instance, are there students in your classroom who feel shame because they live in foster homes, are embarrassed about a hearing impairment, or who have unresolved trauma in their lives that takes up a lot of headspace?

These are the students who especially need your support in learning how to assert themselves. Sadly, some students who feel oppressed will never learn effective ways to have conflict with their classmates. These students are missing out on a learning opportunity. Some of them will drift more and more toward the margins of the classroom unless they learn how to state how they feel and negotiate for what they want. Supporting your students' ability to assert themselves can give them a way to have their voice heard, which can be tremendously empowering.

WHAT DOES THE RESEARCH SAY?

Children tend to rely on three main strategies to resolve conflict: negotiation, coercion, and disengagement (Gadke, Tobin & Schneider, 2016; Laursen, Finkelstein & Betts, 2001). Negotiation is a solution-oriented strategy involving direct communication about a disagreement with an attempt to create a compromise. Research suggests that it is a healthy way to deal with interpersonal conflict. Coercion is a control-based strategy. Although it involves direct communication, it includes persistent arguing and the attempts of one person to control the outcome of a situation, which leads to subordination. Coercion is not a healthy response to conflict. Disengagement is a non-confrontational response to conflict that includes indirect strategies such as hiding angry feelings or withdrawing from the disagreement. For the most part, disengagement is not considered a healthy way to resolve conflict; it has been linked to low leadership capacity and low social competence (Laursen et al., 2001).

What predicts the use of some of these strategies over others? Children's age and personality, their cognitive, social, and emotional skills, the behavior of the other person in the conflict, the nature of that relationship (e.g., sibling or peer), and aspects of the classroom and cultural environment in which students live all contribute to a person's choice of strategies. Here, I shed some light on research about just a few of these factors.

In early childhood, coercion reigns supreme as the most common approach to resolving conflict. As typical children approach age five or six, they use less coercion and more negotiation than before. Disengagement is the least common strategy used by children. By adolescence, youth use more negotiation than coercion or disengagement, and they tend to be about equal in whether they choose coercive or disengaged approaches to handle conflict (Laursen et al., 2001).

The good news is that coercion, the most negative conflict resolution approach, declines as children develop in the first decade of life. Unfortunately, even though coercion is less prevalent, it can be more toxic than ever during the adolescent years because of the way it is contagious among peers. When an adolescent is coercive and aggressive toward another person, they are much more likely to get support from their peers for those negative behaviors. Those peers, in turn, are more likely to be aggressive toward the initial victim of the coercive behaviors, which can lead to depression, loneliness, anxiety, and other negative consequences (National Academies of Sciences, Engineering & Medicine, 2019; Wang et al., 2020). For this reason and others, elementary school is a critical time for students to learn positive conflict resolution skills.

Other factors matter contribute to children's choice of conflict resolution. Students with more agreeable personalities are more likely to disengage rather than negotiate (Gadke et al., 2016). Friendships are relationships that we elect to have whereas siblings are more permanent in our lives. Perhaps for that reason, people are more likely to use negotiation with friends but a mix of negotiation and coercion with siblings (Laursen et al., 2001).

Teachers matter. Classrooms in which children were taught norms related to compassion for others, fairness, and cooperation were more likely to espouse prosocial goals and behave less aggressively in conflict situations than those without such training (Frey, Nolen, Van Schoiack Edstrom & Hirschstein, 2005). Children's empathy and prosocial behaviors have been linked to positive outcomes in conflict situations (Spivak, 2016).

Further, cultural considerations are important for interpreting which conflict resolution strategies are the most valued. Negotiation is a confrontational strategy, whereas disengagement is a nonconfrontational approach. Some cultures value maintenance of relationships such that disengagement may be considered a healthier approach for managing conflict than negotiation. One study tested this hypothesis in Chinese fifth-graders by examining negotiation versus disengagement in response to peer bullying. Contrary to expectations, those students who disengaged from conflict were lonelier than those who used negotiation (Wang, et al. 2020). New research in Latinx young adults describes a cultural attribute called simpatía, which describes a tendency to have positive social interactions while also avoiding conflict and overt negative behavior (Aceveda, Herrera, Shenhav, Yin, & Campos, 2020). A student high in simpatía holds the belief that one should not create conflict and that if someone is being impolite or rude, it is best to ignore it. A child raised in a family high in simpatía may find it aversive to confront others when they disagree. As a teacher, it will be important to know as much as possible about your students and their families. You can incorporate positive, yet non-confrontative approaches to conflict resolution into the classroom or discuss explicitly with students that the conflict resolution strategies at school may differ from those at home, but that you value both.

Teaching Conflict Resolution

Ask Students to Recall a Conflict

To start, ask students to think about a time when they had a conflict with someone. Discuss a few of their ideas about how they resolved the conflict. Consider what happened, with whom the conflict happened, how they handled it, whether the solution was successful, and whether they came to an agreement or not. Ask your students to think about how they moved past the conflict. For instance, in the example at the beginning of the chapter, the students did not move past the conflict in the time-out room. Only when they were getting ready to play soccer together did they get to a new place in the process. Ask your students to talk about how they resolved their conflicts and write a few of these ideas on the board or on chart paper for everyone to see and reflect upon.

Define Conflict and Conflict Resolution

Explain that conflict is a normal part of group work, especially when people feel passionate about a project or about their ideas. A conflict is a disagreement or argument between two or more people. Explain that when you have a conflict, the goal is to resolve it, which means you need to settle the conflict or find a solution to the problem. A resolution is the actual solution that you come up with to solve a problem or conflict.

Describe a Five-Step Process to Resolve Conflict

Share a conflict resolution anchor chart similar to the one shown in Figure 8.1. Use this chart to give an overview of the five-step process of resolving conflict. Many of these steps involve revisiting the skills described in earlier chapters in this book. Still, applying these skills and putting them together into a string of activities is what you are trying to teach. I recommend going through these five steps briefly with your students and then spending time thinking carefully about each step.

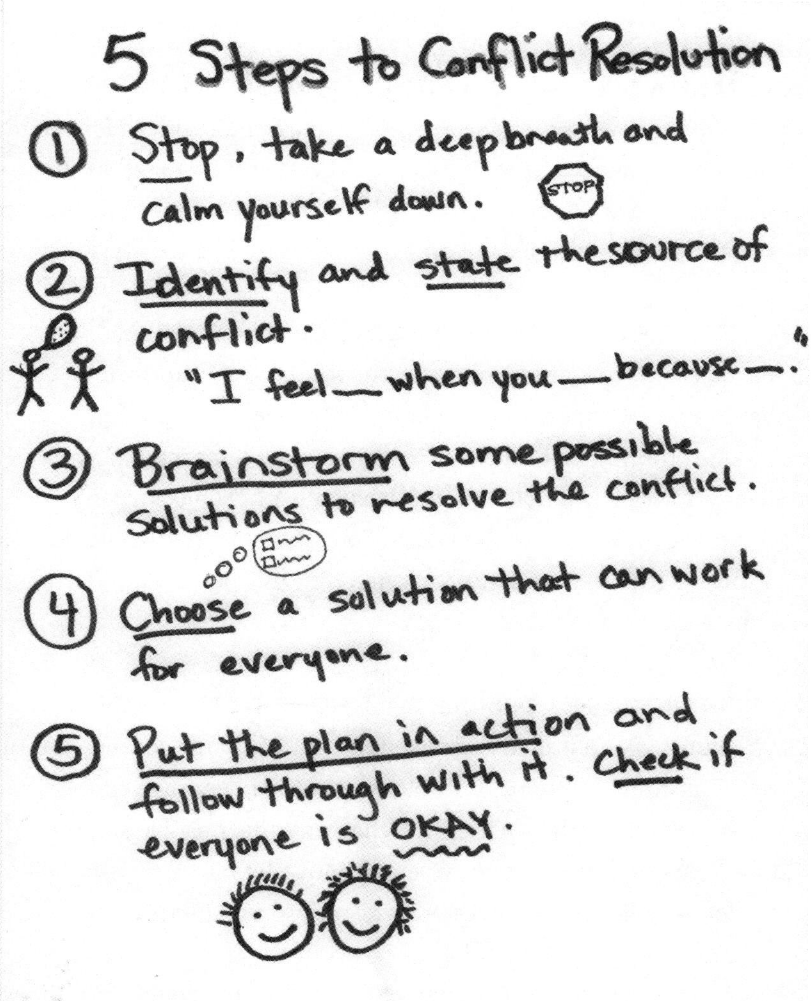

5 Steps to Conflict Resolution

① Stop, take a deep breath and calm yourself down. (STOP)

② Identify and state the source of conflict.
"I feel ___ when you ___ because ___."

③ Brainstorm some possible solutions to resolve the conflict.

④ Choose a solution that can work for everyone.

⑤ Put the plan in action and follow through with it. Check if everyone is OKAY.

FIGURE 8.1. Example of an anchor chart depicting the five steps of conflict resolution.

STEP 1: TAKE A DEEP BREATH AND CALM YOURSELF DOWN.

The first step involves taking a deep breath and calming down. Here, remind students of the strategies that you identified earlier to manage strong emotions in Chapter 5. A glitter jar, stress ball, or take-a-break chair are all ways students can muster up the calm and courage to resolve the conflict.

STEP 2: IDENTIFY AND STATE THE SOURCE OF CONFLICT.

The second step is to identify and state the source of the conflict. Of course, this step cannot be done until a student is calm. Help your students see that they can find the source of the conflict by asking themselves, "Why are we disagreeing?" "What is it that you each need or want?" Once they have found the source, they can state it. Mention to your students that I-statements are useful during this step and explain that you will be learning about and practicing I-statements shortly.

STEP 3: BRAINSTORM POSSIBLE SOLUTIONS TO THE PROBLEM.

After students have identified and stated the sources of the conflict, it is time to brainstorm some solutions to resolve the issue. Encourage your students to ask themselves and their partner, "What are some positive solutions that could make us both content so we could move forward on the work?" (If your students are unfamiliar with brainstorming, explain that it involves no criticism, just the generation of lots of possibilities. If you do not think this will get out of hand, tell your students that it is okay to come up with some silly solutions with their partners, too, because that means they will laugh with their partners, which can relieve some tension.)

STEP 4: CHOOSE A SOLUTION THAT CAN WORK FOR EVERYONE.

Ask your students to look over the solutions and tell each other which solution they would like to choose. This may be straightforward or this may involve a bit of discussion. Help your students understand that the first solution that they choose might not work. Then they should move on to another solution.

STEP 5: PUT THE PLAN IN ACTION AND CHECK IN
WITH EACH OTHER TO MAKE SURE ALL IS OKAY.

Have your students put their plan into action and follow through with it. Too often, a group comes up with a solution and implements it but stops halfway instead of taking the solution all the way to the end. Then, the group concludes that the solution did not work, and new conflicts emerge. Let's avoid that. This final step requires full implementation of their plan. Afterward, it is good for students to check in with one another to see if they were okay with the solution and the way things turned out. This is the kind of conciliatory gesture that brings closure to a conflict.

Introduce I-Statements

Now that you've given an overview of conflict resolution, it is a good time to discuss I-statements. This critical part of conflict resolution teaches students an effective way to assert themselves. "I-statements" which are sometimes called "I-messages" come from the Gordon Model and fit naturally into Step 2 of the conflict resolution process (Gordon, 1975; Gordon & Burch, 2010). Students can use "I-statements" to communicate what another person is doing and how those actions are affecting them in a way that does not blame the other person.

An I-statement looks like this:

> *An "I" Statement uses these words:*
>
> I feel _____ when you _____ because _____.

In Mad Lib format, an I-statement would look like this:

> *An "I" statement uses these words:*
>
> I feel _____ when you _____ because _____.
>
>   (feeling state)   (action of another person)   (source of the problem)

Explain that an I-statement is a statement that you can use to express your feelings in a conflict. Show your students how they can use an I-statement to describe how they feel and explain why their partner is making them feel that way. Convey that I-statements are a great way to communicate what is bothering them without putting the blame on someone else.

Remind your students that when they hear someone use an I-statement, it is important to listen carefully, because it takes courage to use those I-statements. It means that a person in their group is taking a risk and going out on a limb to do their best to resolve a problem. Ask your students to listen in a way that shows that they care about the other person because that person is a member of your community. (The adult version of this idea is to assume positive intent.)

Practice I-Statements

Using I-statements requires practice. Give students a handout with a few scenarios and ask them to prepare I-statements and practice them with another student. Below are some sample conflict scenarios. Use the first scenario as an example and come up with an I-statement as a class. Then, give subsequent scenarios one at a time and have students practice using I-statements in pairs. You can turn this into a handout that students work on in pairs to deepen their understanding and give them practice in using these skills.

- A group member always arrives late each time you meet.
- One person in your group does not get their share of the work done. You have to complete the work for him.
- When sharing ideas, one member always insists that her idea is the best.
- One group member likes to be the leader. However, she keeps telling everyone what to do without listening to ideas from the rest of the group.
- One group member is always busy working on other assignments or drawing during group work. He doesn't want to participate in anything.

If there are common conflicts that come up in your classroom, you can create scenarios based on those situations. Make sure the scenarios are anonymous so that students do not feel targeted unfairly in this conversation.

Ask your students to think about why it might be difficult to use I-statements. Some students will talk about how feelings of frustration make it hard to use them. Discuss calming down before trying to solve a conflict. Other students will say (with annoying confidence), "Because I know that I'm right and my partner is wrong." For this, remind your students that different people have different feelings about the same issue—even at the same moment. Still others may say, "These statements can be hard because the other person can be mean and I feel a little shy around her. I don't want to make her angry." In this case, discuss the importance of using I-statements in the classroom to help you create an environment where everyone has a chance to learn and be a part of the community. Keep in mind that some students may live in environments where I-statements can get them in trouble at home or in their neighborhood. In that case, you can discuss how I-statements are important in the classroom but help them see that different rules may apply elsewhere.

Remind students that it can take time and practice to learn to use I-statements. Also, tell them that everyone in the class needs to learn how to accept I-statements. (Some skills learned about giving and receiving feedback may be helpful here.) It is a great time to mention the norms and remind each other about shared goals for how the classroom should feel.

Give Students Practice Resolving Conflicts

Divide students into groups of three or four and give each group a scenario to resolve. You may want to go over one of these examples as a class first so that you can help them figure out what is causing the problem and give some examples of strategies that can be used to solve it.

Here are some scenarios to try. (You can print out scenarios and give them to students on little slips of paper.)

- Three students are working on a newsletter to families about what they have been doing in their math class. Two team members are goofing around and not helping. The other team member starts to get frustrated.
- Four students are making a poster with news about new families who are coming to their community as refugees from Angola and the Democratic Republic of Congo. One team member shares an idea, and the rest of the team does not like the idea and tells her so. Now that team member moves her chair away and will not participate anymore.
- Four team members are planning an energy fair. Someone needs to talk to the principal to get permission to use the cafeteria after school some night. No one wants to be the one to talk to the principal.
- A group of students is brainstorming ideas for a social studies skit. One member of the group is taking control and not listening to any of the other group members' ideas. The other members are getting upset and frustrated because they want a turn to share their ideas.

If you prefer, skip these scenarios and use a conflict that has actually occurred in your classroom. (Just do not use students' names and make sure no one will know which students were involved.)

As students practice, keep the anchor chart posted in a central place so students can refer to it. Your students will need help and close monitoring to make this work. Walk around, sit in, and listen to the groups as they are discussing each scenario. Give them a little coaching as necessary. Jot down the things that you notice that are going well as they practice this skill. Then come back together and discuss behaviors you may have noticed:

- One group had a great strategy for resolving a conflict.
- Another group had a hard time picking a single strategy to try.
- One group got worked up and angry again when they tried to pick a strategy. Then they had to figure out a way to calm down.
- One group had to try three strategies before they found one that everyone could agree upon.

Remind students of the big-picture goal here. You want to have a classroom where all students can learn and feel like what they say matters. Hint (yet again) that conflict is normal and typical when people are working together, so it is especially important to develop skills to resolve conflicts in ways that make people feel like they are a part of the community.

Keep the Anchor Chart Visible in Your Classroom

Use and refer to the anchor chart in your classroom. Remind students to go back to those strategies when problems arise. If students tell you about problems at recess or from the cafeteria, sit down with the small group and support their efforts to use these strategies to resolve conflict. Because you are so busy, it will be tempting just to have the group sit down and use strategies alone without your presence. Most likely, you will need to be involved in their efforts to resolve conflict until they have had plenty of practice with these skills. If students engage in conflict resolution independently before they are ready, you run the risk of having winners and losers, which only exacerbates the problems. So, sit in and listen. Support your students' efforts to calm themselves down, use I-statements, brainstorm, and choose solutions. Monitor the conversation closely and try your best to give as little input as possible but scaffold when you see the conversation go off the rails. Keep the goal in mind—you want everyone to come out of the conversation feeling pretty good about how things were resolved.

Summary: Why Teach Conflict Resolution?

Conflicts are inevitable in your classroom. The goal here is to raise the level of social skills in your classroom so students are able to resolve these conflicts independently. Plus, that culture and sense of community and connection that you work so hard to create will motivate students so that they see why they should try to resolve conflict. Obviously, some students will be better at this than others. It takes time and practice for students to develop conflict resolution skills, and you may need to intervene and remind them to calm themselves down before resolving a conflict, help with their I-statements, and support their efforts as they generate solutions. Often, some students—those that are most dominant—will be completely unaware that there's a problem.

An important insight from bullying research applies here. Apparently, students are more accurate than teachers at reporting the amount of bullying that occurs in a classroom. Students are good at hiding bullying from teachers. The same goes for conflict. Even the most observant and astute teachers may be seeing only the tip of the iceberg. For that reason, it is important to cultivate conflict resolution skills as effectively as possible so that students can begin to use these skills independently.

Not all conflicts can be resolved by students themselves. One first grade teacher, Robin Fox, identifies problems as green, yellow, or red. Green problems are small enough that students can solve them without help from a teacher. If someone isn't sharing the Legos or says she tagged another player at recess but the other student claims he did not feel the tag, that's a green problem. A yellow problem is one that might have initially been green but now requires some adult intervention because a compromise or resolution could not be reached independently. A red problem requires immediate adult help; if someone is crying or injured, it is the kind of conflict that requires adult attention. In first grade, students tend to label all problems as yellow or red, so it is a teacher's role to help them see that some problems are indeed green problems.

Let's think about the story at the beginning of this chapter. Kudos to this teacher for establishing a set of procedures (including a time-out room) to help students manage conflict. Students in this classroom learned ways to calm down, talk over issues that were frustrating, and manage conflict. What stands out is that the two students followed a set of classroom procedures to resolve conflict (including the time-out room), but it didn't work right away. As the student pointed out, they were still mad. But what's interesting here is that it set wheels in motion. After time went by, one boy chose the other for his soccer team. Time needed to pass before complete resolution of the conflict was evident. Keep this in mind. If you teach conflict resolution and feel a bit impatient because it does not seem to work, be patient. Allow time to pass. Watch for delays before actual resolution occurs. Ask students to tell the stories about conflict that they have resolved, and you will see the fruits of your efforts.

STEPS FOR TEACHING CONFLICT RESOLUTION

1. Ask students to recall a conflict.
2. Define conflict and conflict resolution.
3. Describe a five-step process to resolve conflict, including (a) take a deep breath and calm yourself down, (b) identify and state the sources of the conflict, (c) brainstorm possible solutions to the problem, (d) choose a solution that can work for everyone, and (e) put the plan in action and check in with each other to make sure everyone is okay.
4. Introduce the idea of an I-statement.
5. Practice I-statements.
6. Give students practice resolving conflicts.
7. Come back together and discuss.
8. Keep the anchor chart visible in your classroom and refer to it, especially for low-key conflicts that do not require an adult to be involved.

Conclusion:
SEL for the Future

My daughter and I sat in traffic in an urban part of Boston. Waiting. Waiting. Waiting. People were stewing and honking. Meanwhile, we watched two burly men carry a huge, heavy door out of the back of a large truck, across a busy street, up a set of stairs, through an entryway, and into an apartment building. They lifted the weight, stayed balanced on the truck ramp, turned the door in a tight space between the curb and parked cars, and dodged traffic as they crossed the street. As we watched, I began to think of all the social and emotional skills these men needed to do their job. They needed to communicate effectively with one another, assess each other's strengths and limitations, block out the street noise and honking, manage strong feelings of frustration if things did not go as planned, and so much more. Where did they learn these skills? Did they come to the job with these skills in hand? Did their employer size up these abilities when they hired these guys? These were just a few of the questions that came to mind for me.

These men learned their social and emotional skills through the experiences that they accumulated at home, in school, with peers, in out-of-school programs, in their neighborhoods and communities, as well as in other jobs and beyond. At times, teachers or parents taught them the skills they needed. Other times these men learned by trial and error. They honed these skills with friends and the people around them.

As you think about your role as a teacher, the skills you are teaching your students are the exact competencies that they will need now, as well as in the near and far future, to meet the wide variety of challenges in store for them. Some students in your classroom will certainly learn these skills without your instruction and support. Others will not. To function in adult life and contribute to society, people need to listen to one another, wait their turn, be kind to others, and manage their anger. By teaching these skills with intention and energy and creating opportunities for students to practice these skills in your classroom, you are launching your students well.

SEL in Your Classroom

Your students will need all of the social and emotional skills that you can instill. So many facets of life—both inside and outside of school—involve collaborating with people, identifying problems, and working toward solutions. The complexity of problems that students face now (and will face in adult life) makes a strong case for instruction on social and emotional learning. Like all generations, today's elementary school students will be solving tomorrow's world problems. So much rests in their hands—negotiations for peace versus war, the health of planet earth, giving a voice to the oppressed, racial and social equity, and care for the most vulnerable populations (children, people with disabilities, people born to poor families, and the elderly). Teachers boost students in the right direction to cultivate the skills they will need in the future.

With this book, my goal has been to raise your expectations about what is possible in your classroom. Keep in mind that teaching students social and emotional skills has two components: teaching students the actual skills (e.g., managing conflict), and instilling motivation and values that lead students to apply those skills. For instance, managing conflict is a skill, but students will only be motivated to resolve conflict if they value having people who are different from one another in their connected, close community.

Before thinking through a plan for action, I need to add a cautionary note. A classroom that is warm and socially connected without high-quality academics is an empty promise to children. It conveys that their world is okay even if they are not learning in school. Here's an important reality: a positive, caring classroom environment alone will not produce achievement in students. It is essential to hold high and realistic academic expectations for students and use excellent instruction to support students' academic achievement. Unfortunately, a kind environment with weak instruction will not prepare students for the school and life ahead.

Developing Your SEL Plan

I hope by now it is apparent that SEL can be folded into everyday instruction and noninstructional time. Let us hover on the idea of differentiating between goals and strategies to put a plan in place, an idea that I raised in the introduction of this book. Envision and set goals and then choose strategies to reach those goals. As a reminder, your goals are the clear vision that you have in your head that guides your day-to-day, moment-to-moment decisions in the classroom. Strategies are the teaching practices, SEL lessons, and behaviors that you enact on a daily basis that help you strive toward your goals. Goals stay very stable throughout the year, whereas strategies shift as you adapt to respond to curricular demands and adjust to meet students' needs.

Here, I offer some example goals and show how they link to strategies for building SEL. You can use these goals and aligned strategies to start your year or create your own. Taken together, these goals and strategies will elevate the quality of the social and instructional climate of the classroom, and enhance rather than dilute the academic work in your classroom.

GOAL 1: I WILL CREATE A POSITIVE, CARING CULTURE THAT BRINGS OUT THE BEST IN MY STUDENTS.

Every classroom has a culture. Ideally, teachers partner with their students to build a positive culture as they talk about how they all like their classroom to look, sound, or feel in order to help every student succeed. But we all have been in classrooms where the culture emerged without much intentionality or adult guidance, and those cultures are not particularly inviting places to learn.

Here are a few strategies from this book that can help achieve this goal:

- Create norms with your students to create a positive classroom culture (Chapter 1).
- Exercise these norms by discussing them as a class, reminding students to pay attention to the norms, and asking students to evaluate their progress on these norms. Even update those norms in ways that reflect the changing culture of your classroom (Chapter 1).
- Learn as much as you can about your individual students—what motivates them and what makes them mad. (Look carefully at their responses in the lesson on managing frustration and anger in Chapter 5.) Use this knowledge to engage them in the classroom community and their academic work.
- Become aware of individual students' strengths and develop the kind of respectful relationships with students that help them see that you have their best interest in mind. (See Chapter 4 and notice their level of perspective-taking in the lesson on respecting multiple perspectives to understand their level of maturity in social awareness.)

GOAL 2: I WILL TEACH SOCIAL AND
EMOTIONAL SKILLS WITH INTENTION.

Take time for explicit, intentional instruction in social and emotional skills. Start with the simpler skills early in the year and move toward the more complex. Make sure that the instruction is done in such a way that students can practice these skills with easy examples that do not get them worked up emotionally.

Notice the pattern of instruction exemplified in each lesson in this book. Each lesson evokes students' prior knowledge and experience related to a social and emotional skill. Then the lesson gives instruction in the skill. Students have an opportunity to reflect upon and practice the skill. Then, and only then, is it time to integrate this skill into academic learning.

Here are a few strategies as you strive toward this goal:

- In the first week of school, teach students to be active listeners, disagree with others in ways that show respect, and show interest and curiosity when they approach people with ideas that are different than their own (Chapters 2, 3, and 4).
- Next, prepare students to give and receive constructive feedback gracefully and manage strong emotions like anger and frustration. Then teach students even more complex skills such as how to persevere on long-term projects and resolve conflict in group work (Chapter 6).
- Use storybooks because they provide relatable examples and can be

integrated into English language arts instruction (Chapters 4, 5, and 7 offer examples).

Teaching these social and emotional skills deliberately and intentionally takes time. But the time spent up front pays off down the road. One teacher I worked with commented that she was able to ask students to work together in small groups earlier in the year than usual. She noticed that the kids were able to be more independent in their academic group work than she would typically expect. Further, she observed that the kids were more willing to work together with other students in their class "without grumbling," even if they were not friends. Another teacher mentioned how the kids were more accepting of each other and better at communicating about ideas. Yet another teacher talked about how the use of storybooks made the process of learning new skills smoother while addressing academic goals as well. She said that when she used storybooks to teach about a social skill or emotion, her students took the ideas more seriously. These books gave her a bit more street cred and legitimacy in that the students observed that the skills she was teaching were not arbitrary and specific to their classroom. The students thought these skills were genuinely important because "They were in a real book!"

GOAL 3: I WILL CREATE OPPORTUNITIES FOR STUDENTS TO APPLY THEIR SOCIAL AND EMOTIONAL SKILLS TO ACADEMIC WORK.

Take a fresh look at the Common Core, Next Generation Science Standards, and College, Career and Civic Life Framework for Social Studies (or the equivalent standards in your state). The standards link to social and emotional skills in important ways. For example, the Next Generation Science Standards describe eight practices that implicate many social and emotional skills. Asking questions and defining problems requires student initiative, risk-taking, and assertion. Planning and carrying out investigations requires self-control so students can create plans and carry them out. Analyzing and interpreting data requires perseverance and persistence. Further, engaging in argument from evidence requires that students know how to disagree with someone's idea in a way that shows respect.

Here are a few ideas for leveraging social and emotional skills toward academic learning:

- Teach students to apply their social and emotional skills to academic conversations.
- Remind students of the classroom norms so they show respect and caring in their conversations with other students (Chapter 1).
- Identify content that involves discussion of pros and cons of a decision or critical thinking about a text (Chapters 3 and 6).
- Invite students to use their active listening and respectful communication skills as they engage in conversation (Chapters 2 and 3).

- Model the language to use when discussing different perspectives as a whole group before students launch into their small group work (e.g., literature circles; Chapters 2 and 4).
- Facilitate group work.
- Build in partner work in math or small group discussions in reading or literature circles.
- Create a learning activity, assign roles, and encourage students to work in small groups toward a shared goal.
- Teach students how to manage conflict in case it occurs during group work (Chapter 8).
- Encourage students to use their classroom norms as a guide and remind students to respect each other's perspectives and opinions as they work.
- Support students' efforts to persevere, even when the work gets difficult (Chapter 7).
- Build social and emotional skills into rubrics and self-assessments.
- Encourage students to apply their social and emotional skills in project-based learning and/or service-learning.
- Work with students to identify some problems in our world or community that relate to the content in class.
- Design a project together geared toward fixing an important societal problem.
- Encourage students to exercise their social and emotional skills as they collaborate and take action in their community.

Concluding Points

Let's return to the anecdote at the start of the chapter with two big guys carrying a heavy door. At some point, they were just five years old. They were in early stages of learning self-control, developing their self- and social awareness, and learning to cooperate. (At that age, they could work with another student to clean up supplies after an activity, which may be the kindergarten equivalent of the door-carrying scenario.) They picked up some key skills from their energetic kindergarten teachers, then from the terrific teachers who taught them in first grade, and then from their ambitious, determined, and motivated teachers in second, third, fourth, fifth, and so on. No single teacher nor individual lesson taught them all the skills that they needed to know for adult life. They learned from planned and unplanned experiences inside and outside of school.

With this book, my goal has been to raise your expectations about what is possible in your classroom. Children are always learning social and emotional skills via a developmental process that occurs over time and through interaction with the people around them. By holding high expectations for student behavior and creating an atmosphere that contributes to learning for each and every child in your classroom, you are playing a crucial role in this maturational process. You are one important part of each child's progression toward social and emotional competence.

References

Aboud, F. E. (2003). The formation of in-group favoritism and out-group prejudice in young children: Are they distinct attitudes? *Developmental Psychology, 39*(1), 48–60.

Aboud, F. E., Tredoux, C., Tropp, L. R., Brown, C. S., Niens, U., & Noor, N. M. (2012). Interventions to reduce prejudice and enhance inclusion and respect for ethnic differences in early childhood: A systematic review. *Developmental Review, 32*(4), 307–336.

Acevedo, A. M., Herrera, C., Shenhav, S., Yim, I. S., & Campos, B. (2020). Measurement of a Latino cultural value: The Simpatía scale. *Cultural Diversity & Ethnic Minority Psychology*. doi: 10.1037/cdp0000324

Allport, G. (1954). *The nature of prejudice*. Reading, MA: Addison Wesley.

Anderson, M. (2012). *The well-balanced teacher*. Alexandria, VA: ASCD.

Barrett, M. (2018). How schools can promote the intercultural competence of young people. *European Psychologist, 23*(1), 93–104. doi:10.1027/1016-9040/a000308

Benner, A. D., & Crosnoe, R. (2011). The racial/ethnic composition of elementary schools and young children's academic and socioemotional functioning. *American Educational Research Journal, 48*(3), 621–646.

Buhs, E. S., Ladd, G. W., & Herald, S. L. (2006). Peer exclusion and victimization: Processes that mediate the relation between peer group rejection and children's classroom engagement and achievement. *Journal of Educational Psychology, 98*(1), 1–13.

CASEL. (2018). Core social and emotional learning competencies. Collaborative for Academic, Social, and Emotional Learning. Retrieved from http://www.casel.org/social-and-emotional-learning/core-competencies/

Connect Science. (2019). Connect science. Charlottesville, VA: University of Virginia, Arizona State University, Harkins Consulting. Retrieved from https://www.connectscience.org/

Crosskey, L., & Vance, M. (2011). Training teachers to support pupils' listening in class: An evaluation using pupil questionnaires. *Child Language Teaching and Therapy, 27*(2), 165–182.

Curby, T. W., Rimm-Kaufman, S. E., & Ponitz, C. C. (2009). Teacher-child interactions and children's achievement trajectories across kindergarten and first grade. *Journal of Educational Psychology, 101*(4), 912–925.

Denton, P. & Kriete, R. (2000). *The First Six Weeks of School*. Turner Falls, MA: Northeast Foundation for Children.

Durlak, J. A., Weissberg, R. P., Dymnicki, A. B., Taylor, R. D., & Schellinger, K. B. (2011). The impact of enhancing students' social and emotional learning: A meta-analysis of school-based universal interventions. *Child Development, 82*(1), 405–432.

Dweck, C. S. (1999). Caution—praise can be dangerous. *American Educator, 23*(1), 1–5.

Dweck, C. S. (2007). Is math a gift? Beliefs that put females at risk. In S. Ceci & W. Williams (Eds.), *Why aren't more women in science?: Top researchers debate the evidence* (pp. 47–55). Washington, DC: American Psychological Association.

Dweck, C. S. (2015). Carol Dweck revisits the 'Growth Mindset'. *Education Week, 35*(5), 20–24.

Farmer, T. W., Lines, M. M., & Hamm, J. V. (2011). Revealing the invisible hand: The role of teachers in children's peer experiences. *Journal of Applied Developmental Psychology, 32*, 247–256.

Flouri, E., Midouhas, E., & Joshi, H. (2014). The role of urban neighbourhood green space in children's emotional and behavioural resilience. *Journal of Environmental Psychology, 40*, 179–186.

Frey, K. S., Nolen, S. B., Edstrom, L. V. S., & Hirschstein, M. K. (2005). Effects of a school-based social–emotional competence program: Linking children's goals, attributions, and behavior. *Journal of Applied Developmental Psychology, 26*(2), 171–200.

Gadke, D. L., Tobin, R. M., & Schneider, W. J. (2016). Agreeableness, conflict resolution tactics, and school behavior in second graders. *Journal of Individual Differences, 37*(3), 145–151.

Gordon, T. (1975). Teacher effectiveness training, fifth edition. Crown Publishing.

Gordon, T. & Burch, N. (2010). Reprint Edition. Crown Archetype.

Gregory, A., & Fergus, E. (2017). Social and emotional learning and equity in school discipline. *Future of Children, 27*(1), 117–136.

Grütter, J., & Meyer, B. (2014). Intergroup friendship and children's intentions for social exclusion in integrative classrooms: The moderating role of teachers' diversity beliefs. *Journal of Applied Social Psychology, 44*(7), 481–494.

Hamm, J. V., Bradford Brown, B., & Heck, D. J. (2005). Bridging the ethnic divide: Student and school characteristics in African American, Asian-descent, Latino, and White adolescents' cross-ethnic friend nominations. *Journal of Research on Adolescence, 15*(1), 21–46.

Hamre, B. K., & Pianta, R. C. (2005). Can instructional and emotional support in the first-grade classroom make a difference for children at risk of school failure? *Child Development, 76*(5), 949–967.

Harter, S. (2006). The development of self-esteem. In M. H. Kernis (Ed.), *Self-esteem issues and answers: A sourcebook of current perspectives* (p. 144–150). Psychology Press.

Harter, S., Stocker, C., & Robinson, N. S. (1996). The perceived directionality of the link between approval and self-worth: The liabilities of a looking gladd self-orientation among young adolescents. *Journal of Research on Adolescence, 69*(3), 285–308.

Herrmann, J., Koeppen, K., & Kessels, U. (2019). Do girls take school too seriously? Investigating gender differences in school burnout from a self-worth perspective. *Learning and Individual Differences, 69,* 150–161.

Kawabata, Y., & Crick, N. R. (2011). The significance of cross-racial/ethnic friendships: Associations with peer victimization, peer support, sociometric status, and classroom diversity. *Developmental Psychology, 47*(6), 1763–1775.

Kernis, M. H. (2005). Measuring self-esteem in context: The importance of stability of self-esteem in psychological functioning. *Journal of Personality, 73*(6), 1569–1605.

KIDS Consortium. (2011). *Kids as planners*. Lewiston, ME: Harkins Consulting.

Kuo, M., Barnes, M., & Jordan, C. (2019). Do experiences with nature promote learning? Converging evidence of a cause-and-effect relationship. *Frontiers in Psychology, 10: 305*.

Kuo, M., Browning, M. H., & Penner, M. L. (2018). Do lessons in nature boost subsequent classroom engagement? Refueling students in flight. *Frontiers in Psychology, 8, 2253*.

Laursen, B., Finkelstein, B. D., & Betts, N. T. (2001). A developmental meta-analysis of peer conflict resolution. *Developmental Review, 21*(4), 423–449.

Mackenzie, L., & Wallace, M. (2011). The communication of respect as a significant dimension of cross-cultural communication competence. *Cross-Cultural Communication, 7*(3), 10–18.

McArdle, S. (2009). Exploring the development of perfectionistic cognitions and self-beliefs, *Cognitive Therapy and Research, 33*(6), 597–614.

McCormick, M. P., & O'Connor, E. E. (2015). Teacher-child relationship quality and academic achievement in elementary school: Does gender matter? *Journal of Educational Psychology, 107*(2), 502–516.

McDevitt, T. M., Spivey, N., Sheehan, E. P., Lennon, R., & Story, R. (1990). Children's beliefs about listening: Is it enough to be still and quiet?. *Child Development, 61*(3), 713–721.

Mikami, A. Y., Lerner, M. D., & Lun, J. (2010). Social context influences on children's rejection by their peers. *Child Development Perspectives, 4*(2), 123–130.

National Academies of Sciences, Engineering, and Medicine (2019). *The Promise of Adolescence: Realizing Opportunity for All Youth*. Washington, DC: The National Academies Press. https://doi.org/10.17226/25388.

National Center for Educational Statistics. (2018, June 21). A closer look at teacher income. *NCES Blog*. Retrieved from https://nces.ed.gov/blogs/nces/post/a-closer-look-at-teacher-income

Nishina, A., Jakeem A. L., Bellmore, A. & Witkow, M. R. (2019). Ethnic diversity and inclusive school environments. *Educational Psychologist, 54*(4), 306–321.

Norwood, M. F., Lakhani, A., Fullagar, S., Maujean, A., Downes, M., Byrne, J., . . . & Kendall, E. (2019). A narrative and systematic review of the behavioural, cognitive and emotional effects of passive nature exposure on young people: Evidence for prescribing change. *Landscape and Urban Planning, 189*, 71–79.

Patterson, M. M., & Bigler, R. S. (2006). Preschool children's attention to environmental messages about groups: Social categorization and the origins of intergroup bias. *Child Development, 77*(4), 847–860.

Pettigrew, T. F., & Tropp, L. R. (2006). A meta-analytic test of intergroup contact theory. *Journal of Personality and Social Psychology, 90*(5), 751–782.

Rimm-Kaufman, S. E., Baroody, A., Larsen, R., Curby, T. W., & Abry, T. (2015). To what extent do teacher-student interaction quality and student gender contribute to fifth graders' engagement in mathematics learning? *Journal of Educational Psychology, 107*(1), 170–185. doi:http://dx.doi.org/10.1037/a0037252

Robins, R. W. & Trzesniewski, K. H. (2005). Self-esteem development across the lifespan. *Current Directions in Psychological Science, 14*(3), 158–162.

Robinson, J. P., & Lubienski, S. T. (2011). The development of gender achievement gaps in mathematics and reading during elementary and middle school: Examining direct cognitive assessments and teacher ratings. *American Educational Research Journal, 48*(2), 268–302.

Rudasill, K. M., Reio, T. G., Jr., Stipanovic, N., & Taylor, J. E. (2010). A longitudinal study of student-teacher relationship quality, difficult temperament, and risky behavior from childhood to early adolescence. *Journal of School Psychology, 48*(5), 389–412.

Seale, C. (2019, November). Seattle Public Schools' Plan for Math and Social Justice Actually Adds Up. *Forbes Magazine.* Retrieved from: https://www.forbes.com/sites/colinseale/2019/11/23/seattle-public-schools-plan-for-math-and-social-justice-actually-adds-up/#290472f34ac2

Spivak, A. L. (2016). Dynamics of young children's socially adaptive resolutions of peer conflict. *Social Development, 25*(1), 212–231.

Szumski, G., & Karwowski, M. (2019). Exploring the Pygmalion effect: The role of teacher expectations, academic self-concept, and class context in students' math achievement. *Contemporary Educational Psychology, 59*, 1–10.

Taylor, R. D., Oberle, E., Durlak, J. A., & Weissberg, R. P. (2017). Promoting positive youth development through school-based social and emotional learning interventions: A meta-analysis of follow-up effects. *Child Development*, *88*(4), 1156–1171.

Tenenbaum, H. R., & Ruck, M. D. (2007). Are teachers' expectations different for racial minority than for European American students? A meta-analysis. *Journal of Educational Psychology, 99*(2), 253–273.

Therapist Aid (2020). *I-Statements*. Retrieved from: https://www.therapistaid.com/therapy-worksheet/i-statements

Thomas, K. R., Parkhouse, H., Senechal, J., Lu, Z., Faulcon, L., Gorlewski, J. & Naff, D. (2020). Cultural Diversity Professional Development in Schools Survey. Metropolitan Educational Research Consortium. Retrieved from https://scholarscompass.vcu.edu/merc_pubs/111/

Wang, Z., Chen, X., Liu, J., Bullock, A., Li, D., Chen, X., & French, D. (2020). Moderating role of conflict resolution strategies in the links between peer victimization and psychological adjustment among youth. *Journal of Adolescence*, *79*, 184–192.

Wilson, T., & Rodkin, P. C. (2011). African American and European American children in diverse elementary classrooms: Social integration, social status, and social behavior. *Child Development*, *82*(5), 1454–1469.

Children's Literature Cited in the Text

Abdullah, A. R. (2010). *The sandwich swap.* New York: Disney Hyperion.

Arnaldo, M. (2018). *Little brothers and little sisters.* New York: Balzer + Bray/Harper Collins.

Bang, M. (2010). *When Sophie gets angry—really, really angry.* New York: Scholastic.

Bridges, S. Y. (2015). *Ruby's wish.* San Francisco: Chronicle.

Dempsey, K. (2014). *A dance like starlight.* New York: Philomel.

DiCamillo, K. (2009). *Because of Winn-Dixie.* Somerville, MA: Candlewick.

DiSalvo-Ryan, D. (1994). *City green.* New York: Harper Collins Children's Books.

Fleischman, P. (2009). *Seedfolks.* Stuttgart, Germany: Ernst Klett Sprachen.

House, S., & Vaswani, N. (2013). *Same sun here.* Somerville, MA: Candlewick.

Judge, L. (2014). *Flight school.* New York: Atheneum Books for Young Readers.

Miller, W. (1997). *Richard Wright and the library card.* New York: Lee & Low.

Nelson, D. (2003). *The Star People: A Lakota story.* New York: Harry N. Abrams.

Speare, E. G. (1958). *The witch of Blackbird Pond.* New York: Houghton Mifflin Harcourt.

Spires, A. (2014). *The most magnificent thing.* Tonawanda, NY: Kids Can.

Thompson, L. A., & Qualls, S. (2015). *Emmanuel's dream.* New York: Schwartz & Wade.

Index

Abdullah, A.R., 58
academic learning
    leveraging social and emotional skills
        toward, 156–57
active listening, 21–33
    create visual representation in, 26–27,
        27f, 31
    described, 22–24
    modeling of, 24–26, 28, 30–31, 103–4,
        106
    paraphrasing in, 27–28, 31
    practicing in, 28, 29, 31
    reasons for teaching, 31–33
    reflection as group in, 29–31
    teaching, 24–33, 27f, 30–31
    using, 30, 31
A Dance Like Starlight, 124

anchor chart, xxxiv
    in conflict resolution, 144–45, 147
    in respectful communication, 41–48,
        42f
    with sentence stems, 101–2, 106
    in teaching perseverance, 118–20, 119f,
        122
Anderson, M., xiv
anger
    thermometer representing, 82–84, 83f,
        87
anger management, 74–90
    ask students to generate strategies for,
        85–87
    reasons for teaching, 88–90
    share story about feeling, 80, 87
    teaching, 79–87, 83f

Arizona State University
  Mary Lou Fulton Teachers College at, xiii
Arnaldo, M., 59–60
assertiveness
  in conflict resolution, 130–35
awareness
  self-, xxii
  social, xxi

Because of Winn-Dixie, 59, 70
behavior(s)
  impacting classroom norms, 7–9, 17
Bridges, S.Y., 125
buy-in from students
  in classroom norms, 12, 17

CASEL. *see* Collaborative for Academic,
  Social and Emotional Learning
  (CASEL)
chart(s). *see also* anchor chart
  in emotion management, 85–87
City Green, 60
classroom(s)
  SEL for the future in, 150–58 (*see also*
    social and emotional learning (SEL))
classroom culture
  persevering, 120–22
classroom diversity
  communication and, 51–73 (*see also*
    respecting multiple perspectives)
  value of, 56–57
classroom goals, xxix
classroom norms, 1–20
  behaviors impacting, 7–9, 17

benefits of, 3–5
build into daily life, 15–16, 18
case example, 1–2
confirm buy-in from students in, 12,
  17
create broad categories in, 7–8, 17
described, 3–4
establish, 6–18, 11*f*
generate excitement about year ahead
  in, 6, 17
generate student ideas in, 6–7, 17
idea of consensus in, 9–10, 17
introduce, 6, 17
reasons for, 18–20
reflect on, 13–15, 17
revisit, 12–13, 17
rules *vs.,* 19
write down, 10, 11*f,* 17
classroom strategies, xxx
coercion
  in conflict resolution, 132–35
Collaborative for Academic, Social and
  Emotional Learning (CASEL), xx
College, Career, and Civic Life (C3) Framework for Social Studies, 48, 156
Common Core, 156
communication
  among people who are different from
    you, 51–73 (*see also* respecting multi-
    ple perspectives)
  classroom diversity and, 51–73 (*see also*
    respecting multiple perspectives)
  respectful, 34–50 (*see also* respectful
    communication)

conflict(s)
ask students to recall, 135–36, 147
defined, 136, 147
resolving, 127–47 (*see also* conflict resolution)
conflict resolution
anchor chart in, 144–45, 147
ask students to recall conflict in, 135–36, 147
assertiveness in, 130–35
brainstorm possible solutions to problem in, 137*f*, 138, 147
check in with each other in, 137*f*, 139, 147
choose solution that can work for everyone in, 137*f*, 139, 147
defined, 136, 147
described, 128–29
five-step process in, 136–39, 137*f*, 147
identify and state source of conflict in, 137*f*, 138, 147
introduce I-statements in, 139–42, 147
practice resolving conflicts in, 142–43, 147
put plan into action in, 137*f*, 139, 147
reasons for teaching, 145–47
strategies in, 132–35
take deep breath and calm down in, 137*f*, 138, 147
teaching, 135–45, 137*f*, 147
Connect Science, xiv, xix
SEL for, xiv
consensus
in classroom norms, 9–10, 17

constructive criticism, 103–4, 106
defined, 99–100, 106
described, 100–1, 106
in giving and receiving feedback, 94–98
contact
intergroup, 57
within-group, 57
conversation(s)
modeling of, 24–26, 30
Coolman, F., 88
criticism
constructive (*see* constructive criticism)
culture(s)
persevering classroom, 120–22

decision making
effective, xxii
Dempsey, K., 124
DiCamillo, K., 59
disagreement
respectful, 39–41, 40*f*, 47
DiSalvo-Ryan, D., 60
discipline issues
SEL in preventing, xxvi
disengagement
in conflict resolution, 132–35
diversity
classroom (*see* classroom diversity)
respecting perspectives related to, 51–73 (*see also* respecting multiple perspectives)
Dweck, C.S., 113

effective decision making, xxii

Emmanuel's Dream, 124–25

emotion(s)

    defined, 81, 87

    experiencing *vs.* expressing, 76–77

    strong (*see* strong emotions)

emotional skills

    social and, xx–xxiv (*see also* social and
        emotional skills)

emotion management, 74–90

    ask students to generate strategies for,
        85–87

    defined, 76–79

    described, 76–79

    reasons for teaching, 88–90

    talk about, 81–82, 87

    teaching, 79–87, 83*f*

equity, xxi, 71, 151

evaluation system

    SEL in, xxviii

feedback

    access students' experiences with, 99,
        106

    giving, 91–109 (*see also* giving and
        receiving feedback)

    positive (*see* positive feedback)

    receiving, 91–109 (*see also* giving and
        receiving feedback)

Fergus, E., xxi

fixed mindset

    growth mindset *vs.,* 113–14

Fleischman, P., 60–61

Flight School, 125

frustration

    share story about feeling, 80, 87

    thermometer representing, 82–84, 83*f,*
        87

frustration management, 74–90

    ask students to generate strategies for,
        85–87

    reasons for teaching, 88–90

    teaching, 79–87, 83*f*

giving and receiving feedback, 91–109

    access students' experiences with feed-
        back in, 99, 106

    benefits of, 93

    case example, 102–3, 106

    constructive criticism in, 94–98

    described, 92–93

    model listening in, 103–4, 106

    positive feedback in, 99–106 (*see also*
        positive feedback)

    practice, 104–6

    reasons for teaching, 107–9

    reflect as class in, 105–6

    retell joke and reflect in, 104, 106

    room for improvement in, 94

    sentence stems in, 101–2, 106

    teaching, 98–106

giving feedback. *see also* giving and receiv-
        ing feedback

    defined, 92–93

goal(s)

    classroom, xxix

strategies *vs.*, xxviii–xxxii
Gordon Model
    in Teacher Effectiveness Training, 129,
        139–42, 147
Gregory, A., xxi
growth mindset
    described, 113–14
    fixed mindset *vs.*, 113–14

Harkins Consulting, LLC, xiii
Harkins, T., xiii, xiv
House, S., 60

I-messages
    in conflict resolution, 139–42, 147
Innovation and Development grant
    from Institute of Education Sciences,
        xiii–xiv
intergroup contact, 57
I-statements
    in conflict resolution, 139–42, 147

Judge, L., 125

Katz, M., 16
KIDS as Planners, xiii
K–12 Math Ethnic Studies Framework
    in Seattle Public Schools, 71

learning
    leveraging social and emotional skills
        toward, 156–57
    SEL as process of, xxiii–xxiv

    social and emotional (*see under* SEL;
        social and emotional learning (SEL))
Lennon, R., 23
listening
    active, 21–33 (*see also* active listening)
    modeling of, 24–26, 28, 30–31, 103–4,
        106
Little Brothers and Little Sisters, 59–60
Lord of the Flies, 4
Lubetkin, M., 88

Mary Lou Fulton Teachers College
    at Arizona State University, xiii
McDevitt, T.M., 23
McGregor, R., 88
Merritt, E., xiii
Miller, W., 125
mindset(s)
    fixed, 113–14
    growth, 113–14
    growth *vs.* fixed, 113–14
    misconceptions about, 114–15
    in perseverance, 113–15
modeling
    of active listening, 24–26, 28, 30–31,
        103–4, 106
multiple perspectives
    integrate into academics, 70–72
    respecting, 51–73 (*see also* respecting
        multiple perspectives)

negotiation
    in conflict resolution, 132–35

Nelson, D., 125–26
Next Generation Science Standards, xiii,
    48, 156
norm(s)
    classroom, 1–20 (*see also* classroom
        norms)

paraphrasing
    in teaching active listening, 27–28, 31
peer relationship(s)
    quality of, 5
perfectionism, 117–18, 122
perseverance, 110–26
    anchor chart to guiding future work in,
        118–20, 119*f*, 122
    books about, 124–26
    classroom culture of, 120–22
    defined, 116–17, 122
    described, 112
    mindset in, 113–15
    model, 121, 122
    perfectionism and, 117–18, 122
    reasons for teaching, 122–23
    teaching, 115–22, 119*f*
persevering, 110–26. *see also* perseverance
perspective(s)
    defined, 62, 71
    integrate into academics, 70
    multiple (*see also* multiple perspectives)
perspective-taking exercises, 63–65, 64*f*,
    68, 69*f*, 71–72
plastic water bottle–petroleum anecdote,
    xvii–xix

positive feedback, 99–106
    ask students for, 103–4, 106
    case example, 102–3, 106
    defined, 99–100, 106
    described, 100–1, 106
practicing
    in teaching active listening, 28, 29, 31

Qualls, S., 124–25
question(s)
    learn how to ask, 65–67, 71
    in understanding, 42*f*, 44, 47

race and ethnicity, xxi, xxii, xxxi, 57, 70,
    126, 132
receiving feedback. *see also* giving and
    receiving feedback
    defined, 92–93
reflection
    in giving and receiving feedback, 104–6
    on respectful communication, 46, 48
    in teaching active listening, 29–31
relationship(s)
    peer, 5
    teacher–student, 5
relationship skills, xxi
resolution
    conflict, 127–47 (*see also* conflict; con-
        flict resolution)
resolving conflict, 127–47. *see also* conflict;
    conflict resolution
respect
    defined, 62, 71

respectful communication, 34–50
anchor chart in, 41–48, 42*f*
components of, 36
defined, 35, 41, 47
described, 35–36
generate examples of, 45, 47
poll class in, 38, 47
reasons for teaching, 48–49
reflect on, 46, 48
respectful disagreement in, 39–41, 40*f*, 47
sentence stems in, 41–48, 42*f*
teaching, 37–48, 40*f*, 42*f*
respectful disagreement, 39–41, 40*f*, 47
respecting multiple perspectives, 51–73
ask students to write about, 68, 69*f*, 72
defined, 53
described, 53–57
engage in perspective-taking exercises in, 63–65, 64*f*, 68, 69*f*, 71–72
give students opportunity to practice in, 64*f*, 67–68, 72
integrate into academics, 70–72
learn how to ask questions in, 65–67, 71
read and discuss book in, 58–62, 71
reasons for teaching, 72–73
teaching, 58–72, 64*f*, 69*f*
Richard Wright and the Library Card, 125
Rimm-Kaufman, S., 169–70
Ruby's Wish, 125
rule(s)
classroom norms *vs.,* 19

Same Sun Here, 60
science
sentence stems in, 49–50
Seattle Public Schools
K–12 Math Ethnic Studies Framework in, 71
Seedfolks, 60–61
SEL. *see* social and emotional learning (SEL)
self-awareness, xxii
self-control
child's ability to show, xxvii–xxviii
self-esteem
self-worth *vs.,* 96
self-management, xxi–xxii
self-worth
self-esteem *vs.,* 96
SEL plan development, 152–57
goals in, 152–57
sentence stems
in giving and receiving feedback, 101–2, 106
in respectful communication, 41–48, 42*f*
in science instruction, 49–50
Sheehan, E.P., 23
social and emotional learning (SEL). *see also under* SEL
achievement gains through, xxv
approach to teaching, xxvi–xxvii
baby steps in, xxxiii
for Connect Science, xiv
defined, xx

social and emotional learning (*continued*)
  discipline problems prevented by,
     xxvi
  in evaluation system, xxviii
  for the future, 149–58 (*see also* social and
     emotional learning (SEL) for the future)
  goals *vs.* strategies in, xxviii–xxxii
  key ideas to teach, xxxiii
  plastic water bottle–petroleum anec-
     dote, xvii–xix
  as process of learning, xxiii–xxiv
  SEL plan development, 152–57
  skills for, xx–xxiv (*see also* social and
     emotional skills)
  time as factor in, xxv–xxvii, xxxiv
  in your classroom, 150–58
social and emotional learning (SEL) for the
     future, 149–58
  development of plan for, 152–57
social and emotional skills
  achievement gains through, xxv
  defined, xx
  described, xx–xxiv
  development of, xxiii–xxiv
  effective decision making, xxii
  leveraging toward academic learning,
     156–57
  relationship skills, xxi, xxii, 2, 3, 22,
     36, 53, 66, 93, 128, 134
  self-awareness, xxii, xxiii, 3, 53, 75,
     112, 128
  self-management, xxi–xxii, 3, 14, 36,
     76, 93, 112

social awareness, xxi, xxii, 2, 3, 22, 35,
     53, 66, 76, 93, 128, 153, 158
social awareness, xxi, xxii
social skills
  emotional and, xx–xxiv (*see also* social
     and emotional skills)
Speare, E.G., 61
Spires, A., 115
Spivey, N., 23
Story, R., 23
strategy(ies)
  classroom, xxx
  goals *vs.,* xxviii–xxxii
strong emotions
  management of, 74–76, 81–82, 87 (*see
     also* emotion management)
  noticing, 81–82, 87
  read and discuss book that models han-
     dling, 84–85, 87
student–teacher relationship(s)
  high-quality, 5

Teacher Effectiveness Training
  Gordon Model in, 129, 139–42, 147
teacher–student relationship(s)
  high-quality, 5
The Most Magnificent Thing, 115, 117–18
thermometer(s)
  frustration and anger represented by,
     82–84, 83*f*, 87
The Sandwich Swap, 58, 66
The Star People: A Lakota Story,
     125–26

The Well-Balanced Teacher, xiv
The Witch of Blackbird Pond, 61, 70
Thompson, L.A., 124–25
time
    in SEL, xxv–xxvii, xxxiv
Tugel, J., xiv

understanding
    questions in, 42*f*, 44, 47

Vaswani, N., 60
Vislosky, E., 88
visual representation
    in teaching active listening, 26–27, 27*f*,
        31

*When Sophie Gets Angry—Really, Really
    Angry,* 84, 117
within-group contact, 57

About the Author

Sara Rimm-Kaufman, Ph.D., is a Professor of Education at the Curry School of Education and Human Development at the University of Virginia. As director of the UVA Social Development Lab (www.socialdevelopment lab.org), she and her research group have spent the last two decades conducting research on elementary and middle school classrooms with the goal of developing road maps for administrators and teachers making decisions for youth. Dr. Rimm-Kaufman and her team have conducted research on programs including Connect Science, EL Education, Leading Together, Responsive Classroom, RULER, Valor Collegiate & Compass and beyond. In all of her work, she has had a steadfast commitment to understanding how school experiences can boost educational equity. Dr. Rimm-Kaufman has received many grants from National Science Foundation,

Institute of Education Sciences, and private foundations; has authored more than 100 chapters, articles, blogs, and websites; and has spent more than 20 years of teaching undergraduates, masters, and doctoral students pursuing education. Yet, one of her greatest concerns is that researchers have extensive knowledge about social and emotional learning but rarely share it with teachers in an accessible format. This led her to prepare this book for teachers based on work from a newly developed program, Connect Science. For fun, Dr. Rimm-Kaufman enjoys time doing projects and traveling with her family: Sam, Davida, and Larry.